City Breaks
in
Bruges and Brussels

REG BUTLER

In Association with

THOMSON HOLIDAYS

SETTLE PRESS

Text © 1996 Reg Butler

First published by Settle Press
10 Boyne Terrace Mews
London W11 3LR

ISBN (Paperback) 1 872876 48 X

Printed by Villiers Publications
19 Sylvan Avenue
London N3 2LE
Bruges map by courtesy of the Bruges Tourist Office

Foreword

As Britain's leading short breaks specialist, we recognise the need for detailed information and guidance for CityBreak travellers. But much more is required than just a listing of museums and their opening times. For a few days, the CityBreak visitor wants to experience the local continental lifestyle.

We are therefore very pleased to work with Reg Butler and Settle Press on this latest addition to the CityBreak series of pocket guide-books.

Reg Butler has had considerable experience of the Belgian art cities. As a young courier, he conducted ten full seasons of European tours, with regular visits to Bruges, Brussels and Ghent. Since then he has returned many times to Belgium, writing travel articles for British and American newspapers and magazines.

We're sure you will find this book invaluable in planning how to make best personal use of your time.

As well as CityBreaks in Bruges and Brussels, other books in the series cover Paris, Amsterdam, Rome, Florence, Venice, Vienna, Salzburg, Budapest, Prague, Dublin and New York. Thomson also operate to many other world cities from departure points across the UK.

THOMSON CITYBREAKS

Contents

MAPS

Chapter One

Go romantic in Belgium

In a world where progress is multi-storey living in a cage of steel, glass and concrete, Bruges turns its face firmly towards the past. Nothing, but nothing is built unless it totally harmonises with the medieval surroundings.

The result is northern Europe's best-preserved medieval city, rivalled only by Venice. But behind the Middle Ages facade is a 20th-century lifestyle.

Bruges is supreme among the art cities of Flanders. Much of the city is quite unchanged since the 15th and 16th centuries when great painters of the Flemish Primitive School settled here, including Jan van Eyck, Van der Goes, Hans Memling and Gerard David.

The Groeninge Museum displays some of their finest works, comprising one of the world's great collections of the period.

Bruges today has a dream-like character: an intricate web of canals, crossed by the hump-backed bridges - *Brugge* – from which the city's Flemish name is derived. Pleasure boats cruise along waterways which are lined with mellow 15th-century walls. Some bridges are so low that passengers must crouch down in the boat to avoid damaging the masonry with their heads. Hundreds of swans float peacefully on Minnewater, the Lake of Love.

Cobbled streets are lined with gingerbread houses. There's delight in venturing down little side turnings, to make your own discoveries.

Alleys lead into courtyards and sanctuaries such as the Begijnhof, where lace-coiffed women lived as a self-supporting community.

Bruges, located in the north of Flanders, is not a large town, even though it's the fifth largest city of Belgium. Many corners still preserve the serenity of a village. An estimated 120,000 inhabitants include the residents of the surrounding parishes.

The maritime link

Bruges is only 15 minutes by road or rail from the Belgian coast, and has always had close ties with the sea: initially along the River Zwin, later by a 19th-century canal to the port of Zeebrugge.

From the 13th to the 15th century Bruges was among the leading centres of trade in northern Europe, with a special enclave reserved for members of the Hanseatic League. During that time, merchants from 17 other European nations lived in Bruges. The traders – Flemish and foreign – built beautiful houses with their wealth, which came mostly from the wool trade.

In particular, the dealers of Bruges imported raw wool from England, which played an important part in the Flemish cloth industry. As the hub of the wool and textile business, Bruges thrived for many years. Other trade goods were Russian furs, fruit from Spain and Egypt, cloth from Italy and the Orient, metals from Poland and Bohemia, coal from Britain, and wines from the Rhine valley.

Bruges also prospered as a medieval financial centre, and opened up the world's first Bourse for currency exchange. As a powerful seat of the Counts of Flanders and a favoured resort of the Dukes of Burgundy, Bruges attracted a brilliant group of artists to glorify the great mansions, churches and public buildings.

However, from being such a very rich city in the Middle Ages, Bruges afterwards went to the other extreme and became very poor.

Economic collapse

The decline dated from the end of the 15th century, when the river Zwin - Bruges' direct link to the North Sea - silted up. The city was cut off from waterborne access to the North Sea, and its lucrative wool trade collapsed.

The rival city of Antwerp took over. Men of enterprise and capital deserted Bruges, which became a ghost town.

The English connection

Besides the early trading links with England, Bruges has also rated several paragraphs in English history. William Caxton lived in Bruges for a 35-year period, 1441-1476, in business as a trading agent for English wool merchants.

For a year he was in Cologne, where he learned the craft of printing. Returning to Bruges, he set up a press, and printed his first book in 1474. Two years later he returned to England and started the Caxton press.

Two kings of England have lived in exile in Bruges. In the 15th century, Edward IV spent time in exile as the guest of his personal friend the Lord of Gruuthuse (whose mansion is now a major Bruges museum attraction). When Edward IV returned to England, he honoured his host with the title of Count of Winchester.

During four years, 1656-1659, Bruges was a safe haven for the future Charles II. He spent part of his exile in raising the famous regiment of the Grenadier Guards, with their red coats and black bearskins.

They came over to England at the Restoration in 1660, and stayed. That's how several Flemish military words entered the English language, including 'tattoo'.

When the industrial revolution spread throughout Europe from 1760 onwards, nothing happened in Bruges. The locals had no capital or initiative to tear down old buildings and erect factories instead. Bruges continued to stagnate.

Bruges la morte

By the 19th century, nearly half the population of Bruges was destitute and dependent upon charity. Bruges was a dead city – described as *Bruges la morte* – although British travellers on their pilgrimage to the battlefield of Waterloo rediscovered the town and its faded charm.

Bruges was a cheap place to stay. Retired people from England - usually soldiers who had returned from service in the Far East - found they could live here more comfortably on their pension. An expatriate British colony flourished until World War I put Bruges behind the German lines.

Luckily the town was spared during World War II – perhaps thanks to the sheer lack of industrial targets. In more recent decades, tourism has become the city's principal source of income.

Nowadays, Bruges is admired for its well-preserved medieval architecture, while the ancient canals and the original street patterns are still intact. So many other European cities have magnificent monuments and historical sites, but mostly they are lost between modern buildings. Bruges forms an unblemished entity. Effectively, the poverty of past centuries has become the riches of today.

Even in the smaller details, Bruges has kept its medieval style. Some years ago the asphalt along the roads was replaced by the original type of cobblestones, despite opposition from the bicycle lobby. But the mayor responsible for the policy said "In a medieval city like Bruges, not only the gables and the facades should be beautiful but also the roads and pavements."

Likewise, the city has avoided Amsterdam's mistake of allowing car parking beside the canals. In Bruges, cars and coaches are banished from the streets, except for access. The very few on-street parking places cost £11 for a morning or an afternoon.

Medieval perfection

All this explains why Bruges is one of Europe's loveliest cities. The city has it all: a Belfry which was rebuilt in 1280; the oldest Town Hall in Belgium, dating from 1376; the Basilica of the Holy Blood where a Crusader relic has been kept since 1149. Everywhere you look, there's enchantment.

Bruges by night offers another magic, along streets where outdoor neon signs are forbidden, and lighting comes from wrought-iron lanterns.

There is good choice of restaurants for a celebration dinner. Romantics then go clattering over the cobbles in a horse-drawn carriage, and admire the canalside reflections of floodlit monuments.

Bruges offers many ways to pack a city break with interest, romance and a touch of luxury. You can enjoy the medieval world in 20th-century comfort.

The Brussels contrast

As the capital not only of Belgium, but also of Europe, Brussels is supremely modern. It thrived from independence in 1830 and was rapidly transformed during the rest of the 19th century.

City walls were razed and converted into broad boulevards, the first railway stations were built and the River Senne was covered over to make more highways. At the turn of the century, beautiful Art Nouveau buildings were erected.

After World War II – when Brussels escaped damage – the city's new role as capital of Europe and headquarters of NATO led to a big influx of multinational corporations and international institutions, all requiring highrise office towers.

But the heart of the city around the ancient city square has been kept intact, together with a sedate area of gracious buildings and museums close to the Royal Palace. There is good sightseeing within a short radius of Central Station – and also fine restaurants and traditional taverns.

Chapter Two

Arrival in Belgium

2.1 Choice of routes

By air to Brussels: The principal airline services from Britain are operated by Sabena, British Airways and British Midland. Belgium's national carrier operates the most frequent flights – from Heathrow, Manchester, Bristol, Glasgow, Edinburgh, Leeds/Bradford, Newcastle and London City. Travellers on Sabena's services from Heathrow are given complimentary refreshments in the pre-boarding lounge.

British Airways flies from Heathrow, Gatwick, Manchester and Birmingham; British Midland from Heathrow, Birmingham and East Midlands.

On arrival at Brussels airport, come out of the Customs area, turn left and pass through to the adjoining section of the airport where an escalator goes down to the Airport City Express. A ticket to Brussels Central costs 85 BF, or 120 BF first class.

The train stops at Brussels North after 15 minutes, and at Central after 19 minutes. There are three trains an hour, leaving at 9 minutes, 24 minutes and 46 minutes past every hour from 6 a.m. till midnight.

As you come into Brussels from the airport, away to the right there's a brief distant view of the Atomium. Around Brussels North is an area of skyscraper development, which the locals call Manhattan. But that is outside the main central ring where the tourist interest is concentrated.

The Bruges connection
The onward train to Bruges stops at all three Brussels stations – at 17 minutes past every hour at Brussels North, 4 minutes later at Brussels Central, and 3 minutes later at Brussels Midi.

On the return journey from Bruges, alight at Brussels North for the 15-minute journey to the airport. If you want to do some Brussels sight-seeing, either on the inward or outward journey, alight at Brussels Central and leave your bags at the Left Luggage desk.

By train via Brussels: Eurostar services through the Channel Tunnel have made Brussels and Bruges far quicker to reach than in former times. London Waterloo to Brussels Midi takes 3 hours 15 minutes, while the onward train to Bruges is a one-hour journey. Another possibility is to alight at Lille and catch a motor coach service to Bruges.

There are dedicated Eurostar link services from Edinburgh with stops at Newcastle, Darlington, York, Doncaster, Newark and Peterborough; also from Manchester via Stockport, Crewe, Stafford, Wolverhampton, Birmingham New Street and Birmingham International, Coventry, Rugby and Milton Keynes. A Eurostar terminal is also available at Ashford, Kent.

By car: Whether you travel by car ferry or Le Shuttle, Bruges is only 90 minutes from Calais, thanks to a motorway which avoids the coastal resorts.

Ferries also operate by Sally Line from Ramsgate to Ostend and Dunkirk; or – a much longer journey – from Hull to Zeebrugge on North Sea Ferries.

Bruges is not a car-friendly city. Every effort is made to discourage unnecessary traffic within the city centre. There are many one-way streets, and a 20 mph speed limit. Only a few hotels have parking space. Otherwise drivers can just drop their luggage, and then park underground or out at a ring road parking lot. On-street parking is very limited, and very expensive. Tour coaches are banned, except to drop their clients at a pre-arranged hotel or restaurant.

2.2 Bruges orientation

Central Bruges grew during the Middle Ages, before the time of city planning and grid layouts. The essential city is egg-shaped, ringed by a waterway that acted like a moat around the ancient ramparts. The heart of Bruges is the Market Square area and the Burg.

In octopus style, eight main streets radiate to the original bastion gates, of which four have been preserved. Otherwise only the city gate names remain. Outside the line of the waterway is the 20th-century ring road.

Everything is very compact. All the major sights are within a few minutes' stroll, with visual delight every step of the way. The street scene itself is a living museum of architecture, with gothic details, renaissance, baroque, rococo and neo-classic side by side. Instead of gazing at shop windows, look up to the facades above, which still retain their original style.

Guided tours
Although the main sites are easy enough to find and explore, a guided walking tour can add greatly to the enjoyment. There are hundreds of tiny details which can be brought to life by a professional guide. All these details can be found on your own, but it would take many weeks.

There are two guide associations in Bruges, with about 300 to 400 members. They are all fully qualified, having taken a 2-year course before getting a license. A 2-hour guided tour costs 1,200 francs. Although relatively expensive for one or two persons, it is very reasonable if split among a small group. In high season, individuals can join guided visits that start from the Tourist Office every afternoon at 2 p.m. Cost is 120 BF per person, under-12s free.

To get your bearings with an overall circuit of the highlights, a 50-minute mini-bus tour leaves from the Market Square on the hour every hour from 10 a.m. onwards. Last buses go at 4 p.m. in winter Dec-Feb; 7 p.m. in high-season Jul-Sep; 6 p.m. in the shoulder months. Seats are fitted with headphones, so that you can choose your language for the recorded commentary. Cost is 330 BF, or children 200 BF.

Regular public mini-buses ply across the centre, for a standard fare of 40 BF. A one-day pass costs 100 BF; or you can buy a 10-ticket deal for 260 BF, which can be shared between two or more people. But remember that almost the entire area of tourist Bruges can be easily reached on foot. There is really very little need of public transport.

Another possibility, to explore Bruges itself and the surrounding countryside, is bicycle hire. Reckon 250 BF per day; 150 BF for half day; 70 BF per hour. There is choice of mountain bikes and tandems, though you'd be hard pushed to find a mountain to climb in Flanders. Guided bike trips are available at 450 BF for a half-day.

Independent travellers could save their sight-seeing legs by hiring an electric golf cart for leisured tootling around the quiet streets.

Easily the most popular sightseeing is by boat along the canals, through the most picturesque parts of the inner city. Commentaries can be in three or four languages, which can be somewhat irritating. But the scenic viewpoints are fabulous. The standard cost is 170 BF for the half-hour trip, children 4-11 half price.

Another possibility is a horse-drawn cab tour, starting from the Burg. In the early post-war years, there were only five horse carriages in operation. Now it's thirty, thanks to the growth of tourism. The bowler-hatted drivers look quite

Edwardian, but their tariffs are completely up-dated: 900 francs for a 35-minute circuit, and a tip is expected. So reckon a thousand.

To save on street cleaning, every horse is fitted at the rear end with a stretch of canvas to catch the droppings. A very practical arrangement: nosebag at the front, garden fertility at the rear, and one horse-power in between.

There's also the option of trips by horse-tram, starting from 't Zand (at the bottom of Steenstraat). Reckon 200 BF for a 45-minute circuit.

If you need a taxi, the meter starts at 80 BF. From the railway station to the centre of town would cost between 200 and 300 BF. Tipping is not obligatory. The tariffs are structured to give the drivers a fair living, not dependent on tips. But if the driver is more than usually helpful, or you're extremely happy at having found a taxi when it's raining, a tip is in order.

2.3 Bruges as a base

Even though Bruges is so full of sightseeing potential, it's still worth allotting some time to explore the other highlights within easy reach. With its excellent road and rail connections, Bruges is an ideal base for exploring northern Belgium. A 15-minute train journey goes to the heart of Ostend, right beside a tramway that serves the entire 40-mile coast of Flanders-on-Sea. See chapter 9.

Inland, a 24-minute journey brings you to Ghent – more built-up than Bruges, but with a great historic centre. See chapter 7.

If time permits, Brussels itself is worth at least a full day. Take the train to Brussels Central station, which is only a five-minute downhill walk to the Grand'Place, rated as the most beautiful city square in Europe. See chapters 8 & 9.

On a more sombre historic note, there are half-day coach tours to Flanders Fields, visiting the battlefields of World War I, including Passendale, Hill 60 and the Menin Gate at Ypres.

1 – **Burg**: Tourist Office; Old Recorders House; Blinde Ezel Street (to Fish Market); City Hall; Basilica of Holy Blood; Breidelstraat (to Belfry); Provost's House

2 – **Market Square**: Provincial Government Palace; Post Office; Wollestraat (to Dijver); Belfry; Halles; Steenstraat (shopping area); St Armandstraat (for restaurants); Breydel & Coninck statue

3 – **Vlamingstraat**: Theatre; House Ter Beurze; Akadamiestraat; Hanseatic area

4 – **Jan Van Eyck Square**: Poorters Lodge; Old Customs House; Canal to Potterie Hospice & Damme Gate

5 – **Fish Market**: for good views

6 – **Huidenvettersplein**: Tanners Square

7 – **Rozenhoedkai**: for best viewpoint

8 – **Dijver**: Canal and College of Europe

9 – **Groeninge Museum**: Flemish masters

10 – **Brangwyn Museum**: Art nouveau

11 – **Gruuthuse Museum**

12 – **Church of Our Lady**

13 – **St John's Hospital**: Memling Museum & St John Visitor and Exhibition Centre

14 – **Walplein**: Straffe Hendrick Brewery

15 – **The Beguinage community**

16 – **Minnewater**: 'Lake of Love'

17 – **Powder Tower**

18 – **Ghent Gate**

19 – **Cross Gate**

20 – **St John's House Windmill**

21 - **Jerusalem Church**: Lace Centre; Folk Museum

22 – **St Sebastian's Archers Guild**

23 – **English Convent**

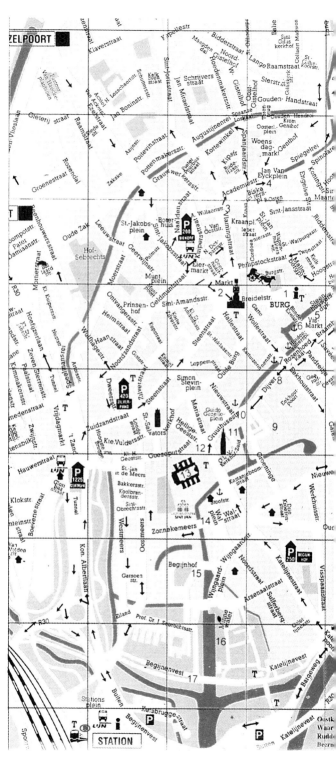

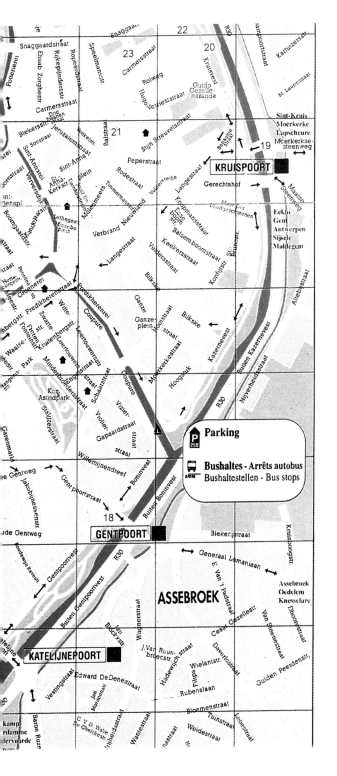

Chapter Three
The historic centre

3.1 The Burg

The history of Bruges began on the city square called Burg (*see map, fig. 1*), which means Castle. Around 862 AD, Baudouin Iron-Arm, the first Count of Flanders, built a new fort around the existing market town.

The stronghold was demolished in 1434, but the name remained. Burg may not be as picturesque as the Grand'Place in Brussels, but is more interesting, with every main architectural style represented around the square.

The group of trees in the Burg marks where Saint Donatian cathedral was founded in 961. The church was an exact copy of Aachen cathedral, with an octagonal ground plan. It was later enlarged in Norman style, then Romanesque, then in Gothic style, but was finally destroyed by the French in 1799.

The church was never rebuilt. But, following excavations in the 1950's, the ground plan has been marked out on the cobbles. With excavated stones, a scale model of the church is displayed among the trees. Part of the Romanesque choir gallery and of the wall of the 10th century fortress is preserved in the basement of the Holiday Inn Hotel.

The City Hall (*see map, fig. 1*) was built around 1400, in Gothic style. It was the first monumental city hall of the Netherlands, and served as a model for many others.

Blind Donkey

Then in the 16th century came Renaissance style, of which the Old Recorders House is a gorgeous example. On top is the statue of Justice, and left and right are two famous judges, Moses and Aaron. The building adjoins the City Hall, separated by an arch that leads over Blinde Ezelstraat, or Blind Donkey Street – so called after a pub of that name that previously stood there.

It referred to the blind justice dispensed in the adjoining Court of Justice. The name of the pub has now been transferred to a restaurant used by workers at City Hall.

The Baroque style of the 17th century is exemplified by the former Bishop's Palace, known as the Provost's House, on the corner of Burg and Breidelstraat (*see map, fig. 1*).

Then came 18th century Classic style, with building of the Court of Justice on the site which originally was the residence of the Counts of Flanders. The building is now occupied by the city administration and the very helpful Tourist Information Office – marked by a large white letter 'i' in a green circle.

Even the 20th century is represented on the square, with a shopping gallery beside the Basilica of the Holy Blood. It's a good example of how Bruges marries 20th century architecture into the medieval city. Likewise, the Holiday Inn doesn't look too much out of place.

City Hall

This superb City Hall was founded in 1376 and completed in 1420. On the ground floor, in the corridor facing the entrance, a number of portraits reflect the varied history of Bruges and its rulers. Among them is the Dutch king William I who reigned from 1815 until 1830, when Belgium gained independence.

The last painting in the corridor depicts the city mayor with Napoleon, who visited Bruges three times. Napoleon was a little fellow, and the mayor of the time, Baron Charles de Croeser, was very tall. But Napoleon is painted the same height. It was unthinkable that a man who ruled over much of Europe could be smaller than the mayor of an obscure provincial city.

Look carefully at the painting, and you can see that at some stage the head of the mayor has been removed. After the battle of Waterloo, the mayor was regarded as a collaborator. So his head was cut from the painting, and hung out of the City Hall in disgrace.

Many more dramatic episodes of local history are displayed in the magnificent Gothic Hall on the first floor. Essentially the hall is cherished as a museum, but is also used for civic receptions, occasional concerts, and a rare banquet when a king or a president comes officially to Bruges. It's a magnificent venue for such occasions. About 700 weddings a year are held here.

During these ceremonies, the hall is closed to the public. Otherwise it is open 9.30 till 12.30, and 14.00 till 17.00 hrs. Admission 60 BF.

The Gothic Hall certainly rates as the most beautiful of any in Belgium, and was built 1380-1401 with a magnificent vaulted timber ceiling. The wall decoration was done much later, in 19th century romantic style, when the trend was to portray the glorious past with its history and battles. The paintings represent the great occasions of Flemish history.

The entire left side of the Hall illustrates the Return of the Bruges Army after the Battle of the Golden Spurs, which took place on 11th July 1302.

From the 9th century, Flanders had been a part of France. An uprising against French rule took place in Bruges on 18th May, 1302, when every French soldier in the town was slaughtered.

When the French king heard the news, he sent his army with the flower of French chivalry to reconquer Bruges and to punish the city.

Winning their spurs

But somehow the Flemish side won the Battle of the Golden Spurs – so called, because all the French knights who lay dead on the battlefield (no prisoners taken) were stripped of their golden spurs. About 1000 French nobles perished.

As this is the only battle which Flanders ever won, July 11 is still a public holiday for the Flemish part of Belgium.

The battle was a turning point in history, the first time that infantry had defeated cavalry. Something similar happened a few years later in Britain, when Scottish foot soldiers routed the English cavalry at Bannockburn.

On the left side of the fire-place is the Duke of Burgundy, Philip the Good, who inaugurated the Order of the Golden Fleece in 1430.

On the right is Diederik of Alsace, the crusader Count who went to the Holy Land and brought back the Holy Blood relic to Bruges – see details below.

Higher around the walls is a gallery of counts, countesses, dukes, duchesses, heroes, artists, writers and preachers from Bruges history.

In the adjoining Historical Hall is a museum collection of artefacts and documents. Most interesting is a splendid old map which shows Bruges in 1562. The layout of the streets is virtually identical to that of today, and many of the street names are unchanged. The map also gives an idea of the buildings that stood earlier on this famous square.

Basilica of the Holy Blood

The legend dates from 1150, when the Count of Flanders fought bravely in the Holy Land and was rewarded with a few drops of the blood of Christ, for his help in liberating Jerusalem. The Count brought the precious relic home, and presented it to Bruges for safe keeping.

The basilica is like a double church, built one above the other. The facade is marked by eight golden statues above the entrances. The lower chapel or crypt is 12th century, built in Romanesque style, with very thick walls and very heavy columns. It seems to be heated entirely by hundreds of pilgrimage candles. The principal work of art is the *Virgin with Child*, a wooden polychrome and gilt statue. Dated about 1300, the gothic sculpture is regarded as one of the loveliest in Bruges.

The upper church, where the Holy Blood relic is venerated, is much more spacious. Over the centuries, the relic has attracted large numbers of pilgrims, especially on Fridays when the shrine is exhibited for adoration.

On Ascension Day every year, a Procession of the Holy Blood re-enacts a medieval procession through the streets of Bruges, with authentic costumes.

During the lengthy march past, scenes are depicted from the Old and the New Testament. The procession is played, mimed, spoken and sung, and is improved upon every year, to become a major tourist attraction.

Advance dates for the Procession are: 16 May 1996; 8 May 1997; 21 May 1998.

The Brugse Vrije
In the corner by the Recorders' House and the former Court of Justice is a Provincial Museum which is open daily, 10-12 and 13.30-17.00 hrs, entrance 20 BF.

This minor museum is worth visiting for its incredible monumental chimneypiece in the Aldermen's Room. It is a tribute to the ruler, Charles V, the Count of Flanders who was also the Holy Roman Emperor of the German nation.

The intricate carving was done about the year 1530. An alabaster frieze, set in the black marble of the chimneypiece, depicts the biblical story of Susannah and the Elders. Every remaining square inch of the courtroom is decorated with paintings and tapestries that depict historic figures.

The Lovers

Among the trees of the Burg square (*see map, fig. 1*) is a charming bronze sculpture, erected in 1987, depicting a young couple on their way to get married. Love is blind, so they are both blindfolded. Plainly the lovers are in a great hurry to get to City Hall on time. The girl's lace veil billows out in the slipstream, even though it's made of solid bronze.

On the plinth is the word 'love' written in 53 different languages. The artists who made the sculpture were Stefan Depuydt (the Flemish word for frog) and his wife Amlivia Canestraio (the Italian word for basket-maker). Hence their joint logo: a frog in a basket, beside their signature at the rear of the plinth.

3.2 The Market Square

From the Burg, a short street called Breidelstraat leads to the Market Square (*see map, fig. 2*) and its famous 272-ft Belfry – the landmark symbol for Bruges, like the Eiffel Tower for Paris.

As you walk along Breidelstraat, watch for a narrow alley called Garre, which was a former 'fire street'. In medieval times, a passage was left between houses so that, in the event of fire, a bucket chain could be formed to fetch water from the nearest canal.

Many of these fire streets are still in place. Watch for them when you take a boat ride. Today, the Garre passageway has some charming taverns with a good range of beers. Stroll down there for an evening thirst-quencher or an informal meal, but be careful of the cobblestones.

The two-acre Market Square has been the commercial heart of the city since 1200 AD, and the scene of political gatherings, state processions, tournaments, open-air theatre and hangings. A central statue honours the two men – Jan Breydel and Pieter De Coninck – who led the Flemish revolution of 1302 against the French.

Against Hapsburg rule

Another major historic event followed upon the marriage in 1477 of the future Hapsburg Emperor Maximilian to Mary of Burgundy, who had inherited Burgundy and the Netherlands from her father, Charles the Bold. Aged 18, Mary was very popular, but Maximilian wasn't. Mary died a few years later in a hunting accident.

After her death, there was general disorder and revolution against her Austrian husband's claim to rule the Netherlands. In 1488 Archduke Maximilian was taken prisoner in Bruges, and held captive for three months in Bouchoute House – the attractive 15th century building, still standing, on the west side of the Market Square, at the corner of St Armandstraat.

From there he could watch the beheading of his supporters, including his bailiff and good friend, Pieter Lankhals. Maximilian was set free when a large rescue force approached the city. He stayed for another year in Bruges to hand out punishments and penalties on his former captors.

In the early Middle Ages, before River Zwin silted up, Bruges was a thriving seaport. Ships could enter the city, and were loaded and unloaded in an enormous covered dock called the Water Halles, located on one side of the Market Square. Today that site is occupied by the late 19th-century Provincial Palace, the neo-gothic seat of the Provincial Government of West Flanders. Alongside is the red-brick Post Office.

Two other sides of the square are occupied principally by restaurants and cafés with interesting gable-end facades. Apart from a Quick hamburger restaurant, everything looks in character.

The fourth side of the square is dominated by the magnificent Belfry, the only one of this style in the world. In the Middle Ages, for a city to have a belfry was the hallmark of riches and freedom. Ever since its construction in 1240, replacing an earlier version, the Belfry has been renovated and altered several times.

Exploring the Belfry

Go through into the Belfry courtyard. The so-called Halles underneath and behind the Belfry were used as a covered market from the early 13th century. On one side is a gallery of rather expensive shops. Opposite is used for banquets.

Upstairs leads to a glorious meeting hall with an awesome beam structure, and colourful banners that have come from a number of Flemish cities. This venue is used for exhibitions, festivities and other special events.

Feeling energetic? Pay 100 BF and you can climb the 366 steps up the Belfry. If you reach the top, the reward is a splendid view of the old city. In fine weather, the coast is clearly visible, only 7 miles away.

You will also hear the bells very clearly when they start chiming – every 15 minutes, night and day. During the main summer season, mid-June through September, there are evening carillon concerts from 21-22 hrs on Mondays, Wednesdays and Saturdays; and also on Sunday, 14.15-15.00 hrs. During the rest of the year, concerts are played at 14.15-15.00 hrs on Wednesday, Saturday and Sunday afternoons.

The present carillon dates from 1742-1748, and comprises 47 bells, with a total weight of 26 tons. This carillon was preceded by three older sets of bells.

En route, pause for breath after the first 55 steps to inspect the treasury, guarded by the oldest wrought-iron gate in Bruges.

Back on the Market Square, look at the scale model near one of the fried-potato stalls. The replica helps give blind persons an idea how the Belfry looks. They can access its size by touch, by comparison with the tiny people at the base. They can feel the model bells, the Belfry terrace and other details. Alongside, in Braille, is an explanation in English, French, German and Dutch. An adjacent city plan likewise gives the names of the main streets in Braille.

3.3 Hanseatic Bruges

Leading out of Market Square, directly opposite the Belfry, is Vlamingstraat. (*See map, fig. 3*). This was the medieval Wall Street of Bruges, originally settled by the Italian bankers who spread around Europe during the Middle Ages (to Lombard Street in London, for instance). The street still retains its financial connections, with several bank headquarters.

Look back from Vlamingstraat, and you can see that the Belfry is a leaning tower. The top is about three feet out of perpendicular. It's not like Pisa's Tower, which is sinking on its foundations.

The Belfry was built this way on purpose, so they say, to compensate for the strength of the prevailing winds. But that's probably a story which the architect invented when he discovered that his plans were faulty.

In the early 13th century, Bruges became one of the principal markets of the Hanseatic League and of the English woollen trade. Merchants from Lombardy and Venice brought their products from Italy or India, and returned with goods from England, Russia or Germany. Foreign trading companies set up their offices and living quarters in an international enclave in and around Vlamingstraat.

Look, for instance, at the House of the Genoese at no. 33, where traders from Genoa settled around 1375 to handle an exchange of spices, precious metals and gem-stones for grain and cloth. They stayed until 1516, when the trade migrated to Antwerp.

In the middle of this Hanseatic trading quarter a family named Van der Beurze ran a pub at House Ter Beurze (*see map, fig. 3*) in Vlamingstraat, on the corner of Grauwwerkersstraat. From 1280 onwards, this establishment was a general meeting-place for business gossip and deals among the international merchants.

Inventing the Bourse

Here was developed a system to buy and sell foreign currency. The Exchange was invented, and the Beurze family name went into every European language as the Bourse, Börse or Stock Exchange – and possibly into English as 'purse'. The building has been skilfully renovated by the Bank of Roeslare.

Note there is good value for money in the restaurants along Vlamingstraat and neighbouring streets, especially around the Theatre.

Further along Vlamingstraat, at number 84, a desanctified Jesuit church is now the venue for Bruges Celebrations – a five-course historical banquet which re-enacts the wedding feast in year 1468 of Charles the Bold and Margaret of York, sister of Edward IV.

The three-hour feast includes wine and Belgian beer, with entertainment by minstrels, jugglers, dancers, fire-eaters and knights in shining theatrical armour.

Buffet menus, served by costumed characters, are available at mid-day.

During daytime in the Apr-Oct summer season, the premises also give a 30-minute audio-visual show that covers the period of 1384-1555, during the time of the Dukes of Burgundy. Performances are scheduled on the hour, every hour, 10-17 hrs, with choice of eight languages through headphones. Entrance 190 BF, or 90 BF for the under-11s.

Turn right along Acadamiestraat, where several street names give more reminders that here was the international quarter of Bruges. On the left is Spanjaardstraat – Spaniard Street. To the right is Biskajersplein – Biscayans' Square.

Beyond Woensdagmarkt (Wednesday Market) with its statue of Hans Memling is Oosterlingenplein – Easterling Square, for the people who came from the East, the headquarters of the powerful German Hanseatic traders. But their guildhouse has disappeared, except for the basement.

Poorters' Lodge

Acadamiestraat leads into Jan Van Eyck Square which has a tall metal statue, unveiled in 1878, of the great Flemish master painter.

On this square (*see map, fig. 4*) is the Poorters' Lodge which acted as a club-house in the 15th century for wealthier citizens and foreign merchants. Among their activities, they organised jousts and tournaments. From 1719 the building was used as the Academy of Fine Arts – hence the street name of Academiestraat. Then, at the turn of the century, the Poorters' Lodge was restored to its 15th-century appearance, and since 1910 has housed the State archives.

The Old Customs House on Jan van Eyckplein is distinguished by its beautiful high facade, dating from 1478. The porch carries the Golden Fleece coat of arms of the Lords of Luxembourg. They had the right to levy a tax on incoming ships, which had to stop here to pay their dues before proceeding to the Market Square for loading or unloading in the Water Hall or the Cloth Hall. The neighbouring building with a narrow gable was the guild house of the harbour workers.

As you wander around, look closely at any building activity. Very strict planning laws ensure that the facades are preserved, even if the interiors are totally gutted and modernised. It's the only way to preserve the appearance of the city, without giving up the 20th-century lifestyle. Try to spot a TV aerial or a satellite dish.

Chapter Four
Canalside Bruges

4.1 The best canal views

In a city of such beauty, it's hard to recommend one walk more than another. But top rating goes to a canalside itinerary that also links many of the sightseeing highlights.

If you're starting from the Burg, plunge down Blinde Ezelstraat – Blind Donkey Street mentioned in the previous chapter – the alley beneath the archway linking City Hall and Old Recorders' House. You'll come to a stretch of waterway called Steenhouwersdijk. Blind Donkey Bridge is located where the first bridge was constructed to reach the Burg over a thousand years ago.

Across the bridge is Vismarkt, the Fish Market (*see map, fig. 5*). It was built in 1820, in classic Napoleonic style. The market operates every morning except Sunday and Monday. The original 14th century fish market was held on today's Market Square, but its removal was ordered in 1745 to the present location.

On the quayside facing the Fish Market is a bust of Frank van Acker, who was the mayor of Bruges for 18 years until his death in 1992. He was a powerful man in politics – the son of a former socialist prime minister – and was himself a Minister of State.

Many local people say that the rebirth of Bruges is thanks to Frank van Acker. For he was dedicated to Bruges, loved the city and made it beautiful again.

Beauty in the cobbles

The mayor's cobblestone reform was characteristic. He ordered the removal of asphalt surfacing from the streets of Bruges, and replacement by the original style of cobbles. He acquired the local nickname of Frank Cobblestone.

The cobbles came from the Ardennes. But that quarry is more or less exhausted; so any replacements are now imported from Portugal. Notice how white cobbles are used to mark road arrows, pedestrian crossings, cycle lanes and even the areas for car parking. It saves the annual expense of repainting for the next few hundred years.

Look back across the canal to the splendid rearside view of the City Hall and Old Recorders' House. A short stroll along the quayside towards Groenerei gives a close-up view of two ancient stone bridges – Meebrug and Peerdenbrug. The city's earliest bridges were of wood, but were built of stone from late 14th century. Mellowed by time, virtually all of the city's eighty bridges make superb viewpoints.

Further along the Groenerei, at numbers 8-12, is an almshouse called 'De Pelikaan', with a beautiful facade, and a bas-relief pelican above the entrance. (See below for general comments on the almshouses of Bruges).

Retrace your steps back to the Fish Market, and enter Huidevettersplein – the Tanners' Square (*see map, fig. 6*). In the Middle Ages, the tanners were always a very powerful guild. It's typical that in Bruges they had their own square. The guild house of the tanners was the building alongside today's Duc de Bourgogne hotel.

Making leather was a very thirsty business. So the tanners also had their own pub, which they called The Cow. That's the entrance to the Duc de Bourgogne, with a sculpted cow still in place, just above the door. From such low-life beginnings, it's amusing to think that the Duc of Bourgogne now rates as the most elegant restaurant in town, and probably the most expensive.

Life around the squares

Why does Bruges have so many squares? Like so many medieval cities, nothing was planned in advance. As Bruges expanded as a trading city, people moved out from one square to another, mostly with a street running into each of the four corners. The squares were meeting places, or markets. Over the centuries, the surrounding buildings were adapted to meet the changes of use.

A 16th-century map shows that the Tanners' Square could be closed with a gate at each end. That was a normal arrangement. If enemy troops entered the city, they still had to conquer it square by square, in a medieval version of urban guerrilla war.

The building opposite the Duc de Bourgogne is a restaurant called the Mozarthuis - not because of any historic connection with the composer. It's just that the owner likes Mozart's music.

Next stop: the Rozenhoedkaai, which means Rosary Quay (*see map, fig. 7*). During earlier centuries, rosaries were sold along this quayside. The stone benches were not intended as seats, but to enable the vendors to display their stock.

Here's the spot to take a perfect picture of the most famous corner of Bruges: the canal, overhanging trees, the medieval facades, and the Belfry in the background. The white canalside facade of the Duc de Bourgogne restaurant is part of that view. Early morning, before boats start rippling the water, the canal is like glass and you get twice the Belfry in one frame.

That picture has been used worldwide by Sabena as a poster, with the slogan "Visit Belgium, Fly Sabena". So the view has become virtually a symbol for Belgian tourism.

Dijver is the canalside promenade (*see map, fig. 8*) where every step is packed with interest. Everywhere you look is sheer delight for the eyes. From March to October, a flea market operates on Saturday and Sunday afternoons along the canal bank. The restaurant called Den Dijver specialises in beer cuisine, with almost every item on the menu cooked in beer. The building was originally a baronial mansion.

Next door is Hotel Tuilerieen, converted from another grand and elegant 15th-century mansion. Then comes the College of Europe (*see map, fig. 8*), an international post-graduate centre which offers courses in European studies: especially economics, law and administration. This building likewise is converted from a manor house.

4.2 The museum cluster

The next group of buildings is the principal museum patch. (See the next chapter for details of these museums). A gateway leads to Groeninge Museum (*see map, fig. 9*), the Municipal Museum of Fine Arts.

A garden and a tiny canal bridge connects to Arents Park and the Brangwyn Museum – named after the English art nouveau painter Frank Brangwyn, who was born in Bruges, and who donated many of his works to the city. (*see map, fig. 10*). Opposite the entrance to the Brangwyn Museum, plate glass windows give you a free look at a collection of carriages and sleds.

The third major museum in this group is the Gruuthuse Palace (*see map, fig. 11*), overlooking the waterway and adjoining the Church of Our Lady which rises splendidly in the background.

In this palace resided King Edward IV when in exile during the Wars of the Roses. Don't miss a visit to this noble 15th-century house - details and more history in the next chapter.

Opposite the Gruuthuse Palace is a square and a statue dedicated to Guido Gezelle, a poet born 1830 in Bruges, died 1899. A priest, he was a nature poet in the style of Shelley or Wordsworth. He is one of the great poets in the Dutch language, but has been very little translated.

4.3 Religion and charity

Church of Our Lady - Built between 1250 and 1380, this beautiful church is embellished with blind windows to make the tower look very slender. The brick tower, 395 feet high, is taller than the Belfry, and indeed is the highest brick-built tower in the Low Countries. (*See map, fig. 12*).

The greatest treasure of the church is the *Madonna and Child* – the only sculpture by Michelangelo that ever left Italy during his life. This masterpiece in white marble was bought direct from Michelangelo in 1506 by a wealthy Bruges cloth merchant who paid one hundred gold ducats for the work.

The sculpture displays two styles. The Madonna is medieval, gothic, very much idealised. She looks just like the Madonnas as painted by the Flemish primitives. The child, in contrast, is very realistic, a saucy little fellow.

In this church are buried two Dukes of Burgundy: Charles the Bold and his daughter Mary of Burgundy. Their mausoleums are in the choir gallery, but that's a museum and it costs 60 BF to see these splendid monuments.

Typical of churches for this region, the general appearance of the exterior is gothic, while the interior decoration is baroque. That's because 16th century Flanders was part of catholic Spain. When Luther came with his new religion, Bruges converted to Protestantism and soldiers entered churches and smashed the interiors.

But Spain came back and reconquered the southern Netherlands. So Flanders was obliged to become Catholic again. However, Spain never succeeded in conquering the northern Netherlands, so the Dutch remained Protestant.

That's why there is still a difference of religion between Belgium and Holland. Later, during the 17th century, Our Lady's Church was redecorated in the style of that period. Hence the early baroque altar, pulpit and confession chairs.

St John's Hospital

Directly opposite the Church of Our Lady is the impressive and solid facade of St John's Hospital, which was founded around 1118. (*See map, fig. 13*). The oldest parts of the building date from the 13th and 14th centuries: the hospital entrance, the central wards and the tower. Over the centuries the complex grew, with an attached monastery for friars, a brewery, more hospital wards, and a convent for the nursing sisters.

In 1976 the building's function as a hospital ended, with the medical centre moving to modern premises elsewhere. The sick wards, pharmacy and the chapel form the **Memling Museum** where six of the artist's most famous works are displayed – see details in the next chapter.

Other 19th-century buildings in the complex have been converted since 1990 into a congress and art exhibition centre with four meeting rooms that can accommodate up to 500 people. A 200-capacity restaurant is open to the public. During summer, outdoor tables are set beside the canal.

Almshouses

An attractive feature of Bruges is the number of low-profile almshouses that still function throughout the city. Altogether 47 of these complexes have been preserved from the 15th century or even earlier. The inner courts can often be entered, but obviously the houses themselves keep their privacy.

The main street leading down from the Church of Our Lady and St John's Hospital is called Katelijnestraat, now lined mainly with shops that sell lace, Belgian chocolate and similar goodies.

Several groups of almshouses are located in this area. In an alley off Katelijnestraat 9-19 is the oldest foundation, dating from 1330. There are two almshouse groups in Nieuwe Gentweg at nos. 8-54 and 57-70; and another at Noordstraat 4-14, where you can peek over a low wall at the almshouse named Godshuis De Vos, built 1713.

Paying for almshouses

Some almshouses were financed by guilds such as the masons, the tailors, the bakers or the shoemakers. At Oude Gentweg 126-130, for instance, are Almshouses of the Tailors. But most of the almshouses were built by wealthy benefactors.

There was always a chapel in the complex. The deal was that the poor or the aged lived rent free. But they had an obligation to go every day to the chapel, and pray for the good family that built the accommodation. Rich people founded almshouses in the hope of gaining entrance to heaven through the prayers of others: like everlasting candles being lit to their memory.

Since the French Revolution the almshouses are no longer privately owned. They are administered today by the city's social security system, but are still used for the same charitable purpose of housing the elderly and the poor. But the tenants are no longer obliged to visit the chapel every day.

A typical terrace comprises eight little houses, each like a bed-sit with cooking facilities. In the Middle Ages and later, people didn't have much furniture: just a bed, table, a couple of chairs, and a chest to store their belongings. Now they need more space, and a TV to watch Baywatch.

So the city is adapting these almshouses to 20th century living, enlarging the accommodation. As planning laws forbid any change to the exterior of protected monuments, two houses are merged into one, complete with an indoor toilet instead of an outside shed.

Most of the houses are grouped around little gardens, which formerly were tended by the residents. This job is now undertaken by the parks and gardens division of the council service.

Almshouses are a medieval concept. But they ensure that the elderly are still integrated into society, and keep their independence as long as possible, instead of being cooped in an old folk's nursing home. When they go out, they are into a shopping street, so they can do their own errands. A 'meals on wheels' service caters for those who cannot prepare their own food.

Strong beer

From Katelijnestraat, turn right into Walplein (*see map, fig. 14*), possibly via Walstraat which means Wall Street. On the Walplein is the brewery of Straffe Hendrik - it means Strong Henry. If you're feeling thirsty or hungry, it's a good excuse not only to drink the beer, but also to have a snack and imbibe the atmosphere. A slice of farmer's bread, with ham or cheese or both, costs about 90 to 130 BF, and is very good value for money. The beer costs another 50 or 60 BF.

Straffe Hendrik was originally known as the beer of city hall – not for the employees, but for official visitors. When Bruges gave a civic reception, the city served good beer rather than champagne, supporting a local industry and saving money. The brewery dates from at least 1546. Guided visits are available Apr-Sep 10-17 hrs; and Oct-Mar 11-15 hrs.

Incidentally, throughout this walk, notice that the usual building material is brick. When anyone built a house with natural stone, he was described as being 'stone rich'.

4.4 Beguinage and Minnewater

The Begijnhof or Beguinage (*see map, fig. 15*) is something special. Firstly, it was not a convent. According to research, the first Beguines were widows of Crusaders who didn't return from the Holy Land. The widows grouped themselves into so-called Beguinages. The word comes from Beguine, beggar, the patron saint of the Beguines. They were the first emancipated women in the Middle Ages. Very independent, they lived an austere life and earned a living in Bruges by washing wool in the canal for the weavers guild.

Vineyard of the Lord

The Beguinage of Bruges was founded in 1214, and was given formal recognition in 1245 by a Countess of Flanders, Margaret of Constantinople. It remained a Beguinage until 1927 when the last Beguine died.

Since 1930 the premises have been occupied by about thirty Benedictine sisters. On certain occasions they wear the medieval black and white costume and white cap of the former Beguines.

The approaches to the Begijnhof are called Wijngaardstraat and Wijngaardplein - Vineyard Street and Vineyard Square. That derives from the original name of the Beguinage, which was the Vineyard of the Lord. There are sculpted grapes over the bridge entrance.

Inside the complex is a large grassed court, shaded by lime trees and Canadian poplars, and with a springtime crop of daffodils. It's an ultra-peaceful setting for the whitewashed houses around the square: a dreamy medieval subject for photographers and painters.

After the last war, Winston Churchill came to Bruges and made a painting of the Beguinage entrance. That picture was later auctioned at Sotheby's in London. A Bruges museum director attended the sale, to see if the painting could be bought for the city.

But the price went too high, and artistically the picture wasn't worth the money. People were bidding for the signature, not for the quality of an amateur's painting.

The Beguinage was bought by the city some 20 years ago for the very reasonable price of 10 million francs. But it costs more than that each year to maintain the property.

Next to the entrance is a tiny house museum, furnished in 17th century style to give an idea of how the Beguines lived. There's also a display of fine lace and lace-making equipment. Entrance 60 BF.

A Sunday church service is held at 9.30 a.m.

Minnewater

Adjoining the Beguinage is the widest stretch of open water in Bruges: the Minnewater (*see map, fig. 16*), which formerly was the dock where canal barges to and from Ghent could tie up. At the Šouthern end of Minnewater are the remains of a Powder Tower or ammunition dump dating from 1398 – part of the general defensive system of fortifications built in the 14th century. From the middle of the bridge is one of the best views of Bruges. (*See map, fig. 17*).

Minnewater has two meanings in the old Flemish language. Minne means 'love' (think of the word minstrel, for a singer of love songs); and minne also means 'common'. The authentic translation of Minnewater should be 'Common Water' – a place where the water belonged to everybody, and where boats could stay overnight without paying a fee.

But in this romantic-minded century of tourism, Minnewater is translated as 'the Lake of Love', and people keep quiet about the prosaic alternative name for this former commercial dock. The beautiful setting gives credibility to the more romantic version.

Swans add another picturesque touch to the scene. Their presence dates from 1488, and was a symbolic penalty inflicted on the city by Maximilian of Austria. As mentioned in the previous chapter, Maximilian of Austria was imprisoned during 1488 in a house on the Market Square.

Among the supporters he saw beheaded outside his window was the Councillor for Financial Affairs, very unpopular of course, called Pieter Lankhals. That means Peter Longneck. Appropriately, a swan featured in his coat of arms.

In perpetual atonement for the execution of Pieter Lankhals, the city authorities were compelled to maintain swans on the canals, for ever. These swans are still the city's responsibility. Every morning a workman goes round with a big bag of stale bread to feed them.

Chapter Five
The Big Four Museums

5.1 The arts of Flanders

Entrance fees to the four leading museums of Bruges are: Groeninge 200 BF; Gruuthuse 130 BF; Memling 100 BF; Brangwyn 80 BF. A combination ticket costs 400 BF – a worthwhile investment if you have enough time to visit all four.

During the Apr-Sep season these museums are open daily 9.30-17.00 hrs. During the Oct-Mar period they keep the same basic hours, but close for lunch 12.30-14.00 hrs; and are also closed on Tuesdays.

The Flemish Primitives

First, a few words of background to the Flemish school of painting. In general, from the 11th to the 14th century the most usual form of painting was manuscript illumination. From around 1420, artists in Flanders switched to painting on wooden panels – mostly oak – using oil paint. About the same time, Italian artists were developing the idea of perspective.

The use of oils made it possible to depict still life in the most minute detail, to portray sweeping landscapes, and to represent light and shade and texture. By applying layers of paint, the Flemish artists achieved richly glowing colours that are characteristic of their style.

In sculpture, Flemish artists – unlike the Italians – were much less significant.

Jan van Eyck

The great pioneer of this new oil-painting technique was Jan van Eyck. In the 1420s he was a court painter to the Duke of Burgundy. During the 1430s, while living in Bruges, he perfected the style, using the medium to portray his subjects in the most microscopic detail. His greatest work is the altarpiece in St. Bavon's Cathedral, Ghent, consisting of twenty panels.

The term 'Flemish Primitives' was first used in the 19th century, at a time of newly awakened interest in the medieval past. To the romantic mind, they were the first painters, though mostly they were neither Flemish nor Primitive. Leading artists came from all over Europe to work in Bruges or Ghent – the economic heartland of Europe at the time, ruled by the Dukes of Burgundy. Here in Flanders was money and patronage. 'Primitive' stands for the beginning of the art of oil painting.

Today the term is applied to the school of painting typical of the period between gothic art and Mannerism, in several towns of 15th-century southern Netherlands, including Bruges, Ghent, Ypres and Brussels.

Most of these works are religious, with a high proportion of Madonnas and Child. Much of the interest is in the backgrounds, showing the gates and fortifications of cities, scenes of everyday life in photographic detail, and a myriad items like furniture, and the dress of the time.

There is a magnificent collection of Flemish Primitives in London's National Gallery, but some of the most beautiful paintings of the period are located in Bruges.

The Groeninge Museum displays major works by each of the leading Flemish artists: Jan van Eyck (1390-1441); Rogier Van der Weyden (1400-1464); Petrus Christus (1420-1476); Hugo van der Goes (1430-1482); and Hans Memling (1430-1494); Gerard David (1460-1523); and Hieronymus Bosch (1450-1516).

This 15-room gallery (*see map, fig. 9*) was built in 1930 to house a basic collection that was started by the city's Academy of Fine Arts, which was founded in 1716. Every Bruges artist from that time had to donate a picture to the institution. After a disastrous fire in 1755, a new collection was formed. Purchases and donations have since made the Groeninge Museum one of the world's best collections of Flemish art from Primitive through to Contemporary.

The first five rooms of the gallery are dedicated to the Flemish Primitives, with works by van Eyck in pride of place near the entrance. In the first room is his *Madonna with Canon Joris van der Paele* – the artist's largest work after the altarpiece in Ghent. Displaying his skill in portraiture is a small panel of his wife, Margaretha, dated 1439.

The picture of *Saint Luke painting the Portrait of Our Lady*, is one of four known versions of this theme by **Rogier Van der Weyden**. The original dates from about 1435, and closely follows the style of composition set by van Eyck. Note the realistic domestic interior and the precise rendering of the Flemish town in the background.

Hugo van der Goes worked mainly in Ghent until he entered a monastery near Brussels as a lay brother. Subject in his later years to extreme depression, he painted the *Death of Our Lady* about 1480, in the year before he attempted suicide. Deep grief shows in the apostles' faces.

Hans Memling came from Germany (like van Eyck) and lived thirty years in Bruges. He has a museum to himself – see below – but is represented here by the *Moreel Triptych*, painted on oak panels in 1484. Look at the delicate detail of the gossamer veils of the nuns. Also by Memling are the two exterior wings from a triptych of *The Annunciation*, of which the central panel is located in Vicenza, while the inner panels of the wings are in New York. During the last war, these exterior wings were acquired by Hermann Goering, but they returned to Belgium in 1947.

In room 4 are several pictures by **Gerard David**, who is regarded by art historians as the last of the Flemish Primitives. He came from Holland to Bruges in 1484, and stayed until his death in 1523. His *Baptism of Christ* includes portraits of donors who paid for the work in 1520.

Jan van Eyck was the first Flemish artist to sign his work, and many of his contemporaries and followers remain anonymous, despite their high quality. A number of their works are grouped in rooms 5 and 6.

Although the Museum is mainly distinguished for its rich collection of Flemish Primitives, later rooms in the gallery offer a good selection of art from succeeding centuries.

Jan Provoost (1465-1529) lived in Bruges from 1494. Among his most dramatic works is *The Miser and Death* in room 6. Note also the lively details of *The Last Judgement*. The paintings are highly realistic, but with Biblical scenes set in the contemporary dress and backgrounds of 16th-century Flanders. His *Crucifixion*, for instance, has churches in the background, with nuns looking on.

In the mid-16th century, **Pieter Bruegel** the Elder was the most important figure in Flemish painting. He moved to Brussels in the final six years of his life (1522-1569) and portrayed scenes of everyday rustic lowlife in village settings and landscapes.

The Sermon of John the Baptist is a copy, made in the workshop of Pieter and Jan Bruegel, of which the original, dated 1566, is in the Budapest Museum of Fine Arts. St John in a hair shirt is surrounded by a peasant throng, with cheeky children climbing overhanging trees, all painted with outstanding realism.

In the latter half of the 16th century, Bruges painting was dominated by **Pieter Pourbus**

(1523-1584), who originated from Holland. He followed in direct line from the art of Memling and of Gerard David, but subject to the great influence of Italian painting of the time.

His *Last Judgement* in room 7 was painted in 1551 for the Council Chamber of the Liberty of Bruges, and was inspired by Michelangelo's work in the Sistine Chapel. Two cherubs brandish something like musical horns, using them like peashooters against the lost souls below.

Principally, though, Pourbus was a portrait painter. In a wedding portrait of *Jan van Eyewerve and Jacquemyne Buuck* you can look through the window and see the Crane Square in Bruges - a location which probably hasn't changed much since 1551.

Afterwards the **Claeissins family** – father and two sons – dominated the Bruges market for official paintings into the beginning of the 17th century. They are each represented in room 7 and in several Bruges churches.

In the Baroque period of the 17th century, **Peter Paul Rubens** (1577-1640) was the most outstanding Flemish painter of his day, though he spent much of his early career and training in Italy and Spain until his return to Antwerp in 1608. He is represented in room 9 with a large painting entitled *The Meeting of Jacob and Esau*.

Rubens' great productivity was aided by following the Italian system of workshops. Qualified artists were assigned areas to paint according to the master's sketches. Even Anthony van Dyck worked as an assistant in the Rubens studio.

The golden age of the Flemish School ended with the death of Rubens. During the next two centuries, Flemish painters followed the lead of French art – neoclassics in room 10, impressionists in room 12, 20th-century expressionists including James Ensor in rooms 13 and 14. The Groeninge Museum is the only institution in Bruges with a permanent display of contemporary Flemish art.

5.3 Brangwyn Museum

Frank Brangwyn was an English artist, born 1867 in Bruges. His family went back to London in 1875. From the age of 12 he helped in his father's workshop, making church embroideries. Apprenticed in the studio of William Morris, he learned the craft techniques of stained glass, drawing, painting and tapestry design. Later, as a young designer working in Paris, he was fully exposed to the Art Nouveau movement. He made lengthy journeys to Istanbul, Spain and Morocco.

All these influences are reflected in his distinguished career in many fields of applied art. He worked with the Royal Doulton potteries, and even played some part in the design of Selfridges in Oxford Street. As a frequent visitor to his birthplace of Bruges, he declared himself inspired by the lovely city. He painted many scenes of Bruges, but also of more exotic locations. The upper floor of the museum is dedicated to the world's largest display of Brangwyn's highly varied work, based on a collection of his work which he donated to the town in 1936. Knighted in 1941, he died in 1956 at Ditchling in Sussex.

The museum's ground floor displays lace from the 16th to the 20th century. (*See map, fig. 10*).

5.4 Gruuthuse Museum

This 15th-century palace of the Lords of Gruuthuse offers a picture of the home comforts, furniture and accessories of upper-bracket Flemish families across the centuries. (*See map, fig. 11*).

The great wealth that financed the building of the mansion came from the monopoly rights to sell 'gruit' to brewers of beer. This was a flavouring, consisting of varied dried plants, which was added to medieval beer. Later the gruit was superseded by hops, but the Gruuthuse family still kept a right to levy an excise duty.

Gruuthuse fame and fortune

The family monopoly was granted initially by the Counts of Flanders, and later by the Dukes of Burgundy. It was a huge source of income in a beer-drinking country, and bought great power in the land.

The most famous member of the family was Louis of Gruuthuse (1422-92), who built most of the palace during his lifetime. He was very well up, socially. He was advisor to Duke Philip the Good, and acted as the Governor of Holland, Friesland and Zeeland. He arranged the marriage of Charles the Bold to Margaret of York (the sister of Henry IV). Later he fixed a wedding between Mary of Burgundy, the daughter of Charles the Bold, to the future Emperor Maximilian I of Austria. As mentioned earlier, he also hosted Edward IV during the king's temporary exile in 1471, and was instrumental in financing his return to the throne.

Above the entrance to the palace is a sculpture of the Lord of Gruuthuse, sitting on a horse. Underneath is his device in French, saying: *Plus est en vous*, meaning "There is more in you." In other words "You can always do better."

The museum collection is extremely varied and extensive, formed initially from 1865 by an Archaeological Society in Bruges. An English resident, art critic James Weale, was the curator. When donations and acquisitions reached 2,000 objects by 1875, the city bought the mansion to display the collection in its present spacious setting, 23 rooms on three floors.

There are magnificent Bruges tapestries dating from the 17th century; lovely beamed ceilings; richly ornamental chimneypieces. Furnishings include oak chests, wardrobes, a 16th-century spinet and a fully-equipped kitchen. There are display cases of coins, silver, pewter and pottery, and a specialised collection of goldsmiths' scales.

The armoury houses weapons and a complete range of instruments of torture. There's even a second-hand guillotine that was bought in 1796 for use in Bruges.

On the upper floor are flat-irons and other domestic equipment, spinning wheels and lace (though most has been moved to the Brangwyn Museum); and more pottery and pewter. From a balcony you get superb views of the canal below, with a little bridge and perfect possibilities for rooftop pictures.

A curiosity is a bridge-shaped family chapel that links the Gruuthuse to the choir of the Church of Our Lady next door. In this oratory the family could sit in privacy and watch and listen to the service.

5.5 Memling Museum

There are three main areas to the Memling Museum in Saint John's Hospital (*see map, fig. 13*).

The pharmacy is a delight, filled with bottles containing traditional remedies and concoctions. Some of the jars are antique blue Delft. In cupboards and drawers, various medicinal herbs were stored. The 17th-century dispensary actually remained in use until the hospital closed in 1976.

The sick wards display furniture and paintings that illustrate the hospital's history. At the time of publication of this book, renovation was in progress, with re-opening expected about the end of 1996.

Opposite the pharmacy is the entrance to the hospital church and its adjoining chapel where six magnificent works by **Hans Memling** are exhibited.

Of all the Flemish Primitive painters, Hans Memling is probably the most admired. No other late-medieval painter appeals so forcibly to the imagination.

Born around 1430 in Germany, Memling studied painting in Cologne and Brussels. He became a citizen of Bruges in 1465, and lived there until his death as a very wealthy man in 1494.

The Ursula Shrine

Around one hundred of Memling's works are treasured as masterpieces in the world's greatest galleries.

Of the six Memling works in this church, the most famous is the *Ursula Shrine*. Commissioned by the hospital, the work was completed in 1489, and is considered to be Memling's finest achievement. The reliquary of Gothic design is shaped like a miniature chapel. Incredibly detailed paintings around the sides and gables of the box portray episodes from the life of St Ursula, whose story was a popular legend of the time.

Ursula was a Christian princess from Brittany who was due to be married to a pagan English prince. Ursula consented to the marriage on condition that her future husband should be converted, and that she could travel to Rome and meet the Pope, while accompanied by 11,000 virgins. It was a tall order, especially as the route took her through Germany.

The journey is recorded in six episodes on the long sides of the box. (1) The fleet arrives at Cologne, where Ursula prepares to land with her companions. Cologne cathedral and the city towers can be recognised. (2) Landing at Basle, where Ursula is ashore while her companions wait to disembark. (3) The Pope and his court await Ursula, who kneels on the church steps; and the baptism of the English prince. (4) The Pope accompanies the maidens on their return to Basle, with the escort winding through an Alpine pass. (5) A camp on the Rhine shore near Cologne, with avid soldiers pouncing on the virgins, who are vainly defended by knights in shining armour. (6) The final scene of general massacre and martyrdom.

The composition and the colours are brilliant. It's tempting to spend all one's time, studying the details of this incredible work. But there are five more Memlings to absorb, all superb, including a large triptych *Marriage of St Catherine*.

Chapter Six

Lesser-known Bruges

6.1 City walls and windmills

Minnewater is located on the southern end of the egg-shaped city, which for many centuries was ringed by ramparts that dated from 1297-1300, with additions in the 17th century. Defensive gates controlled each bridge that crossed the surrounding waterways into the city.

Most of the bastion gates were removed in the 19th century, when their strategic function had disappeared, and they were clogging traffic. But four monumental city gates have been preserved. Clockwise around the city, Cross Gate (*see map, fig. 19*) dates from 1297; Ghent Gate (*see map, fig. 18*) from 1336, but mainly 1402; Blacksmith's Gate (Smedenpoort) built in 1367; and Donkey's Gate (Ezelpoort) from 17th century.

The old ramparts around the inner city now form an attractive green belt, ideal for a 4½-mile walk or a cycle ride.

The city windmills

In the north-east of the city, overlooking Kruisvest are three windmills, perched on the ramparts between Cross Gate and the Damme Gate. According to a 16th-century city plan, Bruges at that time had 25 windmills, of which nine stood on the Kruisvest ramparts. By 1879 the overall number had sunk to three. Two of the existing mills have been brought from other locations in Flanders and are not in use.

The bakers' mill

The only working windmill is Saint John's House Mill – Sint Janshuysmolen (*see map, fig. 20*) – located where Rolweg ends at the ramparts. It's the third mill to operate on this site. The first was constructed when the ramparts were built in 1297. That was replaced by a 16th-century mill which was demolished in 1744.

Then a group of 26 city bakers bought the site and constructed the existing mill in 1770. It continued to operate until 1914, when it was bought by the municipality and allowed to fall into disrepair. Finally restored in 1964, the mill grinds away every summer's day whenever there's enough wind.

The town miller shows visitors around, from May to September, 9.30-12.00 and 12.45-17.00 hrs daily except Wednesday. Entrance 40 BF. The museum-mill is closed the rest of the year. There is no admission to the other two windmills, though they make good photo subjects.

6.2 Off-trail Bruges

A visit to this lesser-known corner of Bruges could be combined with the Lace Centre and the Folklore Museum. They are located in Balstraat and Peperstraat in converted almshouses close to Jerusalem Church (*see map, fig. 21*). Also in the vicinity are the premises of the Royal Archers' Guild of St Sebastian, in Carmersstraat, where the English Convent is located.

Jerusalem Church on the corner of Peperstraat was built in 15th century, financed principally by a rich Genoese merchant family named Adornes, who were very active players in the commercial and political life of Bruges.

The church design – unique in Belgium – is a copy of the basilica of the Holy Sepuchre in Jerusalem. The inspiration for this design came from a visit which Anselmo Adornes made to the

Holy Land. He was murdered in Scotland in 1483, and his heart is buried alongside his wife in the mausoleum in the centre of the church.

The six stained glass windows date from the same period – the oldest windows in the city – and portray members of the family and their attendant patron saints.

The Lace Centre

Alongside the church, the family built a dozen almshouses, of which six have survived into the 20th century and are now used as the Lace Museum (*see map, fig. 21*).

Bruges has a long history of lace-making, and the numerous shops around the town keep visitors well reminded of this traditional craft.

Early examples of lace production are displayed in the Brangwyn and the Gruuthuse Museums, while delicate lace decoration and clothing is portrayed in many paintings made by early Flemish artists.

From the beginning of the 18th century, a lace-making craft school was established by a religious order, to give girls a Christian education and a source of income that would keep them off the streets during hard times.

Since 1970, the Lace Centre has taken over the craft-school functions. Various courses are provided in the workshops, and the establishment also acts as an international information centre.

The attached museum covers the history of lace-making, with demonstrations every afternoon. A shop sells lace patterns, bobbins and other requisites. The museum is open weekdays 10-12 and 14-18 hrs; until 17 hrs on Sat; closed Sun. Entrance 40 BF.

Folklore Museum

Close to the Lace Centre, by the corner of Balstraat at Rolweg 40, the Folk Museum is based on half a dozen renovated almshouses. Interiors show the opposite end of the social spectrum from that displayed in the Gruuthuse Palace museum. Fully equipped with traditional tools are separate workshops for a cobbler, a hatmaker and a cooper.

There's an old-time kitchen, classroom, pharmacy, confectioner's and a grocery store. Specialised collections are displayed of pipes, clothing, lace and even baking tins. Very welcome is a working museum-tavern called The Black Cat (De Zwarte Kat) which offers 20th-century refreshment.

Open daily 9.30-17.00 hrs during the Apr-Sep high season. Closes for lunch 12.30-14.00 hrs during the Oct-Mar period, when it also shuts on Tuesdays. Entrance 80 BF. *(See map, fig. 21)*.

The Archers' Guild

In a parallel street to Rolweg, at Carmerstraat 174, are the premises of the Archers' Guild of Saint Sebastian *(see map, fig. 22)*. Prince Charles and the Queen are honorary contemporary members, continuing a long-standing tradition of membership by Belgian and British monarchs.

Charles II signed the visitors' book in 1656, when he and his brother, the Duke of Gloucester, joined the Guild while they were living in exile in Bruges. Since then, every British king and queen has been an honorary member.

The longbow archers launched their Guild in the 13th century. Early members fought in the Crusades and helped defeat the French in the Battle of the Golden Spurs in 1302. The archives go back to 1416. Membership rolls and the accounts can be audited from 1514 onwards. The present building – distinguished by its slender shooting tower – dates from 1573.

The Guild's museum displays numerous trophies of longbow archery. Among the works of art are many portraits of which the oldest was painted by van Dyck in 1641. During the French Revolution the Guild was disbanded and its treasures were sold. But wealthy members bought everything in, and restored the artefacts when the Guild was revived.

The premises can be visited on Mon, Wed, Fri and Sat from 10-12 hrs and 14-17 hrs. Entrance 40 BF.

English Convent

On the same street as St Sebastian's Guild is the 17th-century English Convent (Engels Klooster), founded in 1629, with construction mainly in the period 1647 to 1661. (*See map, fig. 23*). The prioress from 1766 to 1808 was a descendant of Sir Thomas Moore, who lost his head in 1535. Queen Victoria visited here in 1842.

Crossbow guild

While St Sebastian's Guild was dedicated to the longbow, the contemporary St George's Guild was established for practice in crossbow shooting. Their archives date from 1321.

The Guild's existing premises are located at Stijn Streuvelsstraat 59 – close to Jerusalem Church. A small museum features a valuable collection of crossbows, and some good paintings. Open to visitors Mon, Tue, Thu & Fri, 14-18 hrs, entrance 50 BF.

The Potterie Hospice

If you continue a city rampart walk northwards, you'll be rewarded by fine panoramas of the town centre on one side, and tranquil canal views on the other. The most picturesque return to central Bruges is then along the canal quayside called Potterierei.

En route at Potterierei 79 is the Potterie Museum, which is not specialised in pottery but has collections of varied arts and crafts from the 14th century onwards: paintings, sculptures, gold and silverware, manuscripts and much furniture.

This museum is sited in a large hall and rooms of the Hospital of the Potterie. The hospice was founded in the 13th century in this corner of

Bruges where many potters worked. Lay brothers and sisters cared for the poor, the sick and the aged. The premises are still used today as a retirement home for elderly women.

The church contains many fine Bruges tapestries, including *The Birth of Christ*, woven in 1530. In the right aisle is the chapel containing a famed 13th-century white stone statue of Our Lady of the Potterie, who has numerous miracles to her name.

Three tapestries made around 1630 illustrate 18 themes that relate to some of the best miracles, including the rescue of fishermen from a storm, a smallpox cure and the recovery of some stolen dinnerware.

Open 9.30-17.00 hrs, but closed for lunchtime and on Wed. Entrance 80 BF.

Return to base

Follow the canalside walk to the end of Potterierei or Langerei across the water, and you come to bridges that offer the choice of three canalside directions: along Gouden-Handrei to the Hanseatic district described earlier, along Spiegelrei to Jan Van Eyck square, or along Sint-Annarei back towards the Burg.

Chapter Seven

Ghent

7.1 The medieval centre

From Bruges there are four trains every hour to Ghent, a 24-minute journey. Unlike Bruges, Ghent has grown and modernised into a bustling industrial city with 350,000 population. But there are still entire sectors where the 13th to 16th centuries are supreme, with richly decorated gable-fronted patrician mansions.

On arrival at Ghent's main railway station, called St Pieters, take any tram numbered 1, 10, 11, 12 or 13 to Korenmarkt, the tourist heart of the city. *See Ghent map, fig. 1.* Cost is 40 BF single for the 13-minute ride.

Information and walking tours

Close to Korenmarkt is the Information Bureau in the Crypt of the Town Hall (*see map, fig. 2*) on Botermarkt, meaning Butter Market. The office hands out excellent city maps and brochures, marked with several circuits for walking tours.

Every afternoon at 2.30 from Easter till the end of October a two-hour guided walk starts from the Information Bureau, taking in the highlights of the city centre. The cost is 200 BF per person, under-12's free.

A visit to the cathedral is included, but not to the chapel containing the world-famous altarpiece *The Mystic Lamb*, painted by Jan van Eyck (50 BF admission).

GHENT CENTRE

1 - Korenmarkt / Corn Market
2 - Tourist Information Office
3 - Graslei guild houses
4 - Korenlei guild houses
5 - St. Michael's Bridge
6 - Hooiaard / Haymarket
7 - Groentenmarkt / Vegetable
    Market
8 - Grootvleehuis / Meat Market
9 - Former Fish Market
10 - Gravensteen Castle
11 - Museum of Folklore
12 - Vrijdagmarkt / Friday Market
     & Guildhouse of the Tanners
13 - St. Jacobs kerk / St Jacob's
     Church
14 - St. Baafs / St Bavon's Cathedral
15 - Belfry

N

Waterway

0   metres   200

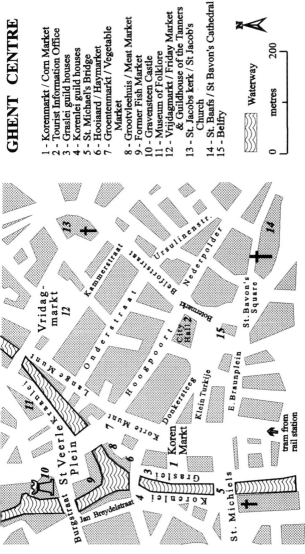

57

Follow the Town Crier

On Sundays at 10.30 a.m., May through September, the Town Crier of Ghent leads a walking tour of five typical Sunday morning markets – flower market, pets, flea market, bird market and arts market.

The tour is free, with no reservation required. The starting point is at the Flower Marketplace called **Kouter**.

Canal boat trips function year-round, costing 150 BF for a 35-minute circuit. For best views and photos, choose the open boats which operate from Easter till the end of October.

Wandering around by yourself, you'll find that most of the sightseeing highlights are tightly grouped within a few minutes' walk of the Korenmarkt – the Corn Market.

Graslei and Korenlei

Rather like Bruges, Ghent enjoyed great prosperity in medieval times as a political and trading centre. Located at the confluence of the River Schelde and the Leie, a network of canals was lined with warehouses. *See map, figs. 3 & 4.*

The heart of the medieval harbour was only a few steps from Korenmarkt, alongside the quaysides named Graslei and Korenlei. Grain was the most important commodity handled.

During the Middle Ages, more than 150 grain storage warehouses packed the centre of Ghent. Many of those Romanesque limestone buildings with their characteristic semi-circular arches still remain, including one from the 12th century.

The grain arrived along the River Schelde from northern France. Ghent had early privileges in corn marketing – a monopoly on sales to other areas of Flanders.

Wherever the ultimate destination, the grain had to pass through Ghent. About a quarter of the annual consignments were for local consumption, and the rest was distributed by the Ghent boatmen.

Weaving through history

Ghent was also deeply involved in the wool and cloth trade, using best quality English wool. Even today, textiles are still the city's principal industry – spinning, weaving and linen manufacture.

The weavers were always an independent-minded group, rioting frequently against taxes and other irritants.

They were also fiercely patriotic in the defence of Flanders – repulsing an English army under Edward I in 1297, and playing an active part in the defeat of the French in the Battle of the Golden Spurs in 1302.

Medieval guild houses

Several guild houses, representing various trades, were located here in the commercial centre. Along the Graslei, a typical building of yellow sandstone dates from the 16th century, and has a sculptured boat at the entrance. That was headquarters of the Boatmen's Guild.

Alongside was the house of the Grain Measurers – grain was sold by measure, not by weight. The lower part was the guild house, with a warehouse above.

The building called **Het Spijker** was originally a grain warehouse. It's now a restaurant, where you can sample a wide range of beers. The intention is to promote 'beer culture', placing regional beers centre stage and educating customers and visitors in the differences in the preparation methods and taste between mass-consumption 'commercial' beers and smaller local beers.

Look across to the other side of the canal, from the Graslei to the **Korenlei**. The white and orange house with dolphins on the facade was another house of the boatmen. Several buildings are either for sale, for rent, or are being converted to new functions.

Note the high roofs, and the hole at the top for a beam to which a pulley would be attached.

This was designed to lift goods to the upper floors of a warehouse. Lower floors were often damp, whereas upper storeys were better for dry storage. Notice, too, that some upper floors have doors that open out above the quayside, not windows.

In early centuries, houses were mainly wooden. From the 16th century it was forbidden to construct in wood, owing to the fire hazard. Many buildings were therefore renewed in brick and stone during the 16th and 17th centuries. The result is a superb mixture of architectural styles and facades from past centuries.

If you stay in Ghent till nightfall, this entire scene takes on a floodlit magic. The best viewing point, night or day, is from **St. Michael's Bridge** (*see Ghent map, fig. 5*), offering sight of Ghent's famed row of towers – St Nicolas Church, the Belfry and St Bavon's Cathedral.

In former times, the street level was much lower. You can see this in a 13th-century warehouse in the **Hooiaard**, which means Haymarket. The building is now used by a line of four small taverns, and customers must go several steps down into the original ground floor.

The food markets

Several market places and covered markets are located in this area. The open-air fruit and vegetable market, the **Groentenmarkt** (*see map, fig. 7*), is still in business every weekday morning, but until the 16th century it was a fish market.

Look across for the shop Tierenteyn-Verlent, which sells only mustard – a speciality of Ghent. The company was established in 1790, and they still follow the same recipe, filling little pots from a wooden barrel. It's an unusual souvenir to take home – small, portable and tasty.

On the canal side of the square is the former covered meat market, the **Grootvleeshuis** (*see map, fig. 8*). This very large building was constructed first in wood and then renewed in grey stone in the early 1400's. It continued in use as a meat market until the 18th century, and then served a variety of other functions.

At the time of writing, this magnificent building with its original oak roof timbers is under reconstruction. For the roof alone it is worth preserving. Renovation may be completed by the end of 1996.

Sint-Veerle Plein

Past the meat market, go left over the Vleeshuis Bridge. A square called Sint-Veerle Plein opens up, dominated by the forbidding presence of the 12th-century Castle of the Counts, the Gravensteen. In the 16th century, the square was used for religious executions.

First, though, look to the corner of the square, which was the covered fish market (*see map, fig. 9*) built in baroque style, 17th century. On top is Neptune, god of the sea, and two large figures, man and woman, who represent the two rivers of Ghent, the Schelde and the Leie.

7.2 Gravensteen castle

An original 9th-century fortress was built here of wood, mainly in defence against the Vikings, and was replaced by a stone building from the 10th century. *See Ghent map, fig. 10.*

Then Philip of Alsace, a crusading Count of Flanders, returned from the Holy Land, having been greatly impressed by the massive style of the Crusader castles. He followed that style to rebuild the mighty fortress in 1180.

In the early 13th century, Ghent became the capital of Flanders, and the principal seat of the Flemish court. At first the feudal castle doubled as a residence, but lacked home comforts. Hence, in the 14th century, the Counts moved to a new palace called Prinsenhof.

The castle was then used for general administration, and as a mint. Later it became a court of justice, which explains the building's dungeons, execution courtyard and a fine collection of instruments of torture.

During most of the 19th century, the castle became a cotton-spinning factory based on a spinning jenny smuggled out of England.

By 1884 the building was redundant, marked for demolition and redevelopment. At that stage, the premises were bought by the state, and reconstruction began.

Since then, Gravensteen has operated as a museum, an evocation of medieval times, and a venue for concerts and public meetings. A detailed exploration of spiral staircases, ramparts, turrets, the Knights Hall, crypt and dungeons can occupy an hour or two. Open daily 9-18 hrs (until 17 hrs Oct-Mar). Entrance 80 BF.

Folk Museum

Also worth a visit is the Museum of Folklore, just a few blocks from the Castle, by the canal along Kraanlei, which means Crane Quay. The Folklore Museum is based on former almshouses from 1363. *See Ghent map, fig. 11.*

With its charming courtyard, the complex was renovated in early 16th century, when new houses were added. The complex was later sold to an industrialist for working class housing, and it finally became the property of Ghent city in 1941. It has been a museum of folklore since 1962.

The rooms show craft and trade activities from the beginning of the 20th century: candlemaking, wood-turning, tin and pewter working and baking. There are house interiors with furniture, an old time barber shop, a chemist; and collections of dolls, musical instruments and old gramophones. A puppet theatre on Wednesdays and Saturdays attracts many children.

Open daily except Mon, 9.00-17.30 hrs Apr-Oct; 10-17 hrs Nov-Mar. Closes for lunch. Entrance 80 BF.

Just past the Folklore Museum – still on Kraanlei – is a shop that sells varied sweets but mainly biscuits called Ghent Mokken, with a cinnamon and aniseed flavour, a speciality of the town. Above the shop is a richly ornamented gable-end, yet another facade worth a photo.

Across a bridge brings you into **Friday Market** (Vrijdagmarkt) which was a meeting place in medieval times for political activists. It was the rallying point for medieval guild members whenever there was trouble. *See map, fig. 12.*

A remarkable character was an ambitious member of the Guild of Brewers named Jacob van Artevelde. A demagogue, he gained great power and was appointed 'Captain of Ghent' in 1337. He was a close ally of the English king, Edward III, in the war between England and France. On this square, he even proclaimed Edward III as King of France,

A bronze statue of Jacob van Artevelde stands on the spot where the proclamation was made. He's in full oratorical mode, delivering the speech which persuaded the local citizens in 1340 to enter an alliance with England. Around the base of the statue are the coats of arms of the all-powerful guilds.

At the back is a commemoration of the union between Flanders and England. The important textile towns - Brugge, Ghent, Koortrai, Ieper - all needed English wool. Edward III was accompanied for the occasion by his wife Philippa, who gave birth to John of Gaunt during her stay in Ghent.

Today, the square is used mostly for parking, but on Friday morning and Saturday afternoon it becomes a busy farmer's market with cheese and meat stalls, full of local character. Flowers are sold around here on most mornings, especially azaleas and begonias. The Ghent region is the world's largest producer of azaleas.

St James Church

The finest building on Friday Market square is the **Guildhouse of the Tanners**, dating from 1480. Close by is **St James Church**, where the tower and the facade from the mid-12th century are Romanesque in style, despite a total restoration in 1870. *See map, fig. 13.*

Numerous antique shops are located in this neighbourhood, and there's a flea market around St James Church on Fridays and Saturdays.

City Hall

From there, Belfortstraat leads back to City Hall (*see map, fig. 2*), built partly in flamboyant 16th century Gothic style, followed later by completion in Renaissance style. The original plan was to make the construction one level higher, but the city ran out of money. The interior has some very fine historical rooms with good paintings.

The City Hall may be flying the flag of Ghent, black with a white lion. Most Flemish cities have a lion as their symbol. Opposite the Tourist Information Office is the Café den Turk dating from 1228 – claiming to be Ghent's oldest café.

7.4 St Bavon's Cathedral

This great cathedral has a very plain exterior, but inside it is one of Belgium's most richly decorated churches, with a remarkable crypt. *See map, fig. 14.* Especially the cathedral is famed for its art treasures, of which the greatest is the *Mystic Lamb*, an altarpiece painted by Hubert and Jan van Eyck between the years 1420 and 1432. The work is considered as the supreme achievement of 15th-century Flemish art.

The van Eyck painting in the Vydt Chapel can be seen during the Apr-Oct season from 9.30 till 12, and 14 to 18 hrs. Or shorter times Nov-Mar. On Sundays, afternoons only. Admission 50 BF.

Rubens is also represented, with his *Entry of St Bavon into the Monastery*, painted in 1623.

The Belfry

Facing the cathedral is the belfry tower (*see map, fig. 15*), which was originally used for storage of documents and as a fire watch tower – very necessary when so many buildings were made of wood.

Also the belfry chimed the hours, because in early days there was no dial on the outside.

Later, more bells were added, so they could play little tunes. Thus started the carillon, which today has 53 bells. Above the bells is a dragon weathervane of gilded copper, the size of a small car and weighing half a ton.

The upper part of the belfry is new, from the beginning of this century – a replacement of the original wood with stone. A lift goes to the level of the watch-tower, offering a marvellous view over the rooftops of ancient Ghent. Entrance 80 BF, or 100 BF with guide.

Art museums

For art enthusiasts, Ghent has a Museum of Contemporary Art and a Museum of Fine Arts in the same building, including paintings by Jeroen Bosch. The location is in Citadelpark, within a short cab-ride of St Pieters railway station.

Industrial heritage

For those more interested in machinery relics, the Museum of Industrial Archaeology (MIAT) tells the story of the transition from an agrarian to an industrial society from the 18th century until the present. The focus is on the cotton industry which gave a magical boost to Ghent in the 19th century. Steam engines and turbines are shown, and complete workshops have been reconstructed. The address is Minnemeers 9. Tel: 09-223 5969. Entrance BF 80.

Chapter Eight
Central Brussels

8.1 Capital sightseeing

Brussels is certainly worth visiting if you have a day or two to spare. If you are arriving by air or train from UK, or taking a side-trip from Bruges, the best starting point is **Central Station**. *See both Brussels maps, fig. 1, on pages 67 or 77.* Don't get out at Brussels Nord or Brussels Midi.

For the principal highlights of the Lower Town, come out of the main exit, cross the Boulevard de l'Impératrice and go through the archway to the left of the Meridian Hotel. Turn down to the right.

Then, opposite the **Galeries Royales Saint Hubert** (*see Central Brussels map, fig. 2*), take the little street that faces on the left, past a bread and pastry shop on the corner, and the main square – the Grand'Place – is straight ahead. It's about a five-minute walk, and you're in the heart of the sightseeing action.

Royal Brussels

The alternative, if you are avid for great collections of ancient and modern art, is to go *behind* Central Station, and walk up steep flights of steps to the **Palais des Beaux-Arts** and towards **Place Royale**. It's about 10 minutes to the Upper Town, depending how much puff you need for all those steps. See details and the orientation map on page 77 in the next chapter.

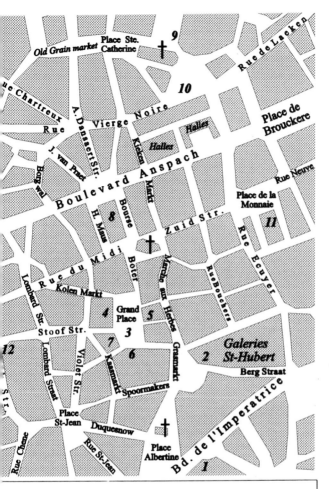

1 - Central Station
2 - Galeries St-Hubert
3 - Grand' Place
4 - Hotel de Ville /
   Town Hall
5 - Maison du Roi /
   City Museum
6 - House of Dukes of
   Brabant

7 - Brewery Museum
8 - Bourse / Stock
   Exchange
9 - Former fish market
10 - Tour Noire /
   Black Tower
11 - Royal Theatre of La
   Monnaie / Opera
12 - Manneken-Pis

0   metres   200

CENTRAL
BRUSSELS

8.2 The Grand'Place

One of Europe's most beautiful city squares is the Grand'Place (*see map, fig. 3*), where ancient guild-houses and civic buildings are ranged around all four sides. Gold-leaf decorations sparkle in the sunshine.

Flower stalls give still more colour to the square, which is also the venue for a Sunday-morning pet and bird market. For several days in mid August, the Grand'Place is covered with a gigantic flower carpet, laid by a team of florists from Ghent, using ten colours of begonias.

There is music and a Sound and Light show every evening from around Easter until the end of September. The floodlit facades look as if they have been made of delicate Brussels lace.

First, some historical background. The original layout of the Grand'Place dates from the 12th century as a marketplace and focus of merchant life. Brussels was a staging point between the port of Bruges and the largest German city of Cologne.

The city's first ramparts were designed to protect the square and the surrounding rabbit-warren of narrow streets. These little streets formed the food district, with their names still surviving into the 20th century – Butter Street, Pepper Street, Herrings, Meat and Bread, Butchers, Herb Market Street...

The whole district forms 'the Sacred Isle', as a reminder that Brussels originally stood on a small island between two arms of the River Senne – later roofed over, and now re-routed.

With the city overflowing its 12th-century ramparts, a second line of fortifications arose in the 14th century. By the 18th century, with still further city expansion, the walls had become a nuisance, and Napoleon ordered their removal.

Today's inner ring boulevard is the only reminder of a defensive wall that encircled the city for 2½ miles, with 42 towers and seven gates. Only four towers still remain, and odd fragments of walls.

The present-day appearance of the Grand'Place is due to a bombardment of the city ordered by Louis XIV in 1695. Training their cannon on the Town Hall spire, the French artillerymen rained 4,000 cannon balls on the city centre. The square and its surrounding wooden houses were set ablaze. About the only building to survive was the Town Hall, damaged but not destroyed.

Out of the ruins a new Grand'Place arose, with the guild houses of the wealthy trade corporations rebuilt in stone, while the streets around were replanned.

In four years the job was done – a masterpiece of flamboyant architecture in Italian Baroque style, with each guild rivalling its neighbour in extravagant decoration. Faithful to tradition, the architects kept the characteristic Flemish gable.

Three centuries later, the square still remains what Jean Cocteau described as "the richest theatre in the world".

Town Hall

Let's look first at the dominant Hôtel de Ville or Town Hall (*see map, fig. 4*) which was built in the first half of the 15th century. The slender 370-ft tower was completed in 1454. To the right of the tower is the Tourist Information Office, on the ground floor. Stop there for helpful information, brochures and city maps, details of special events and the sale of one-day travel cards.

The 'Tourist Passport' costing 220 BF gives unlimited rides on the public transport system, a free map, and reduced price admission to museums and exhibitions. But remember that the central highlights can easily be reached on foot.

Because of the lack of balance to the Town Hall, there is a general accusation that the architect was drunk when he designed it, though the popular judgement seems rather harsh.

Angelic weathervane

There are more statues and windows on one side of the tower than on the other, mainly because the right wing was not added until after the tower was built. Topping the spire is the gilded copper figure of Archangel Michael, the patron saint of Brussels, who doubles as a weathervane.

The interior features a number of fine halls and chambers, with numerous paintings and tapestries – many of historical interest. But admission is limited to Tuesdays at 11.30 and 15.15 hrs; Wednesdays at 15.15; and on Sundays April-September at 12.15 hrs. Entrance 80 BF.

La Maison du Roi

Facing the Town Hall across the Grand'Place is a gothic style building with a spire. Despite its appearance, the Maison du Roi (or the Bread Hall in Flemish) is not a medieval building. It was built at the end of the 19th century, on the original site of a Bread Market. *See map, fig. 5.*

Despite the name, no monarch has ever lived there. Instead, it has been the city museum since 1897.

On the ground floor are rooms with Brussels tapestries, gothic sculptures of the 14th and 15th centuries, and pottery.

Quite delightful is a Bruegel painting depicting a village wedding procession. The bride is very fat and is dressed in black. The husband dressed in green looks deeply unhappy. Bruegel himself lived from 1563 in Brussels, and many of his later paintings depict the surrounding countryside.

The first floor traces the development of Brussels over the centuries, and there are historical paintings on the top floor. On the top-floor landing, a huge processional scene records a very splendid Grand'Place event from the year 1615. In the presence of Archdukes, some soldiers are firing their muskets, officers are riding on horseback, and banners are flying.

The Manneken-Pis wardrobe

Finally, a room on the upper floor is devoted to an amusing display of all the costumes presented over the years for the wardrobe of everyone's favourite statue of Manneken-Pis.

The story goes that this greatly cherished statue was stolen by the soldiers of Louis XV. To make amends, the naked boy was kitted out with the elegant Court dress of a marquis. That was the first item in the Mannikin's wardrobe, and the idea spread. (See directions below, to find the statue in full stream).

The museum is open Mon-Thu 10.00-12.30 and 13.30-17.00 hrs from Apr-Sep; until one hour earlier Oct-Mar. Sat-Sun 10-13 hrs. Closed Fri. Entrance 50 BF.

Guildhouses

Outside in the square, you could easily spend an hour or two in identifying each individual building with its history and original function.

At the top end of the Grand'Place (left when facing the Town Hall) is the House of the Dukes of Brabant, consisting of six separate houses which were reconstructed together in 1698, to give the collective appearance of one palatial building. *See map, fig. 6.*

Each house has a name (left to right): The Purse, The Hill, The Pewter Pot, The Windmill, The Fortune, and The Hermitage.

On the same side as the Town Hall is The Golden Tree at no. 10, the Brewers' House, topped by the equestrian statue of Charles of Lorraine. *See map, fig. 7.* This building is home of the Brewery Museum, which celebrates the Belgian beer culture and includes a fine collection of old tankards, jugs, and the implements of an 18th-century brewery. Opening time is 10-18 hrs, daily except Monday. Entrance 100 BF.

Next door is The Swan – Guild House of the Butchers – where Karl Marx and Friedrich Engels wrote the 'Communist Manifesto' in 1847.

Guild House facades

The most interesting group is at the lower end of the square (right when facing Town Hall). Left to right, The Fox is the Guild House of the Mercers; The Horn is the House of the Boatmen, with maritime decorations including dolphins and a balustrade shaped like a 17th-century ship's prow.

The She Wolf is House of the Archers, one of the finest buildings on the square; The Sack is House of the Coopers and Cabinet Makers, with a sign showing two men carrying a sack; The Barrow is House of the Tallow Chandlers; and The King of Spain is House of the Bakers, with a gilded bust of Saint Aubert, patron saint of bakers.

Altogether, it's an embarrassment of architectural riches!

8.3 Boulevard Anspach

From the Grand'Place take the street beside the Bakers' Guild House. That is Butter Street (Boter in Flemish, Beurre in French - all street names are in both languages). Butter Street comes to the rear end of the Bourse or **Stock Exchange**.

Along the right-hand side of the Bourse are ruins from a church which was first established in 1238. The restored remains have been covered with a glass roof, so that passers-by in the pedestrian precinct can view the excavations from above. *See map, fig. 8.*

The Bourse itself was built about 1870, and is located above a somewhat unsavoury river which was roofed over to make the city's wide central highway – called **Boulevard Anspach** at this point – that goes in a direct line between Midi Station and North Station. Then in 1970 the river was re-routed round the city, and the former river bed has been taken over by one of the important lines of the Metro system.

Pause for a beer

Several statues in plinths around the Stock Exchange were carved by Rodin, who lived in Brussels for six years, during the height of the capital's prosperity. If you're now feeling thirsty for Belgium's national drink, try a Café close by called Beerstreet, at 119 Boulevard Anspach. The bar counter displays 74 beer pumps, each dispensing a different beer.

8.4 Ancient food markets

Opposite the Bourse is **Dansaertstraat**, on the other side of Boulevard Anspach, leading to the old heart and belly of Brussels, where food markets formerly flourished. Attempts are being made to restore the district to its old glory.

The area around **St Catherine Square** (St Katelijne) has some charming old buildings, and leads towards a 16th-century canal which linked Brussels with Antwerp. It's a little-known fact that Brussels is still a port. Here, until 1910, were the docks and the Fish Market, along the **Quai aux Briques** (Baksteen). The quayside is now occupied mainly by expensive and up-market sea-food restaurants. *See map, fig. 9.*

Passing round the back of St Catherine's Church, you'll see one of the few remaining vestiges, the **Black Tower**, of the city's medieval fortifications. *See map, fig. 10.* From there, return to the Boulevard Anspach.

Place de Brouckère

If you have nostalgia for turn-of-the century atmosphere, stop for a coffee at the Métropole Hotel on Place de Brouckère. The hotel and its elegant Métropole Café is worth experiencing for its Art Nouveau interior, even though a cup of coffee costs 90 BF. In this kind of traditional café they often serve a small bar of chocolate with your coffee, to be eaten in between sips.

Shopping precinct

Rue Neuve, which runs parallel behind Place de Brouckère, was the first pedestrianised shopping street in Belgium. It contains shops for average incomes and includes Marks and Spencer.

In the adjoining **Opera Square** is the Royal Theatre of the Monnaie (which in this context means the Mint). *See map, fig. 11.* It was one of the first opera theatres in the world, but its greatest role was to start a revolution!

Song that made history

On 25 August 1830, a performance of Auber's *La Muette de Portici* was presented. One of the patriotic songs inflamed the audience, who rioted out of the show and went looting. The demonstration ignited the 1830 revolution against Dutch rule, and led directly to Belgian independence.

Gourmet restaurants galore

If hunger is now gripping, explore the very narrow street called **La Petite Rue des Bouchers**. As the name implies, it was a former centre of the meat trade, but now it is totally lined with restaurants. If you are planning to have a memorable meal, just wander along and inspect the great choice of menus.

Despite the original meat connection, many of the eating places are dedicated to seafood. Chez Leon, for instance, is Europe's most famous restaurant for mussels, with branches in several other cities including Paris and Moscow.

This little street leads into the splendid glass covered **Galeries St-Hubert**, the first shopping arcade ever built in Europe, dating from 1847. The shops are very stylish. The galleries are split into three - the King's, the Queen's and the Princes' Gallery.

You are then back within a few minutes of Grand'Place or Central Station – or to St Michael's Cathedral.

8.5 Manneken-Pis

How to find the world-famed Mannikin-Piss? From the Grand'Place, take the little street called Rue de l'Etuve (Stoofstraat) that runs down to the left of the Town Hall (*see map, fig. 4*). At the beginning of the street, beneath an archway, is a recumbent male statue, shiny in parts.

He was a 14th-century hero of Brussels who became chief alderman and was later assassinated. The tradition is that unmarried ladies touch the metal to ensure good luck in finding a husband. The monument is highly polished from the constant fingering.

Continue three blocks down that street, which features a large number of souvenir stores, lace shops and outlets for sweets and chocolates, so you know you're on the right trail.

The Mannikin fountain on a street corner (*see map, fig. 12*) has become one of the great tourist legends, enriched by numerous re-tellings. The Mannikin has been performing for visitors ever since he was cast in bronze in 1619 to replace an earlier version in stone. He rates as the most popular citizen of Brussels.

Sometimes he performs nude, but more often is clothed. Around five hundred costumes and uniforms have been presented over the years for the Mannikin's wardrobe, and are exhibited in the Maison du Roi (see above).

The idea is to dress him in appropriate outfit according to a wide variety of national days, or on special occasions for various trades and guilds. A notice board displays his dress programme for the next week or two.

Chapter Nine
Royal Brussels

9.1 The Upper Town

In the Upper Town, the area around Place Royale is totally different in style from the popular and commercial Lower Town. The hilltop has functioned as the residence of royalty and government since the 11th century, from the Dukes of Brabant to the present-day king of Belgium.

On the slope of the hill, the gothic **Cathedral of St Michael** (*see map, fig. 2*) has undergone reconstruction which has revealed remains of the original 12th-century church. As the cathedral of kings, princes and dukes, the building has been a long-standing witness to the history of Belgium.

Numerous royal and ducal figures across the centuries are commemorated in paintings and stained glass. The mausoleum of the Dukes of Brabant behind the High Altar is surmounted by a 3-ton gilded copper lion, cast in 1610. Entrance 40 BF.

On Coudenburg Hill, in the neighbourhood of Brussels Park, the architecture is classical. The **Palais de la Nation** – the Houses of Parliament (*see map, fig. 3*) – was built in 1779 by a French architect.

Facing the Palais de la Nation, across Brussels Park, is the **Royal Palace**. The central block dates from 1827, with two 18th-century wings. The building occupies the site of the chateau of the Dukes of Brabant, burnt down in 1731. A palace visit may be possible during summer.

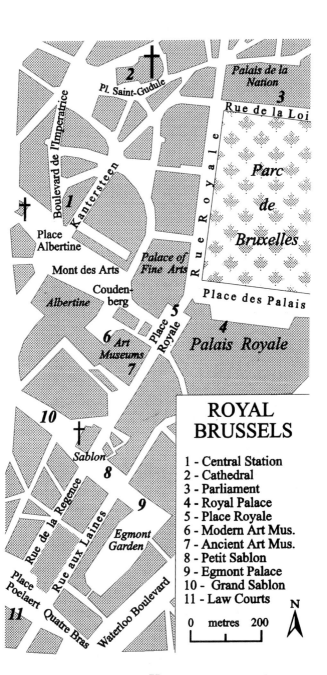

2 Pl. Saint-Gudule

Palais de la Nation
3

Rue de la Loi

Boulevard de l'Impératrice

Kantersteen

1

Place Albertine

Mont des Arts

Albertine

Couden-berg

Palace of Fine Arts

Rue Royale

Parc de Bruxelles

Place des Palais

5

Place Royale

4
Palais Royale

6 *Art Museums*

7

10

Sablon

8

9

Rue de la Regence

Rue aux Laines

Egmont Garden

Place Poelaert

Quatre Bras

Waterloo Boulevard

11

ROYAL BRUSSELS

1 - Central Station
2 - Cathedral
3 - Parliament
4 - Royal Palace
5 - Place Royale
6 - Modern Art Mus.
7 - Ancient Art Mus.
8 - Petit Sablon
9 - Egmont Palace
10 - Grand Sablon
11 - Law Courts

0   metres   200

N

Ranged along another side of the park is the **Palais des Académies**, a 19th-century neo-classical building that houses the Academies of Science, Letters and Fine Arts.

The park itself, and the area around Place Royale (*see map, fig. 5*), saw fighting against the Dutch during the Revolution of 1830. So it was appropriate that Leopold, the first king of independent Belgium, was crowned in the Place Royale itself.

In the centre of **Place Royale** is a statue of Godefroid de Bouillon, departing on horseback for the first Crusade. He is surrounded by 18th-century buildings including the Church of St. Jacques sur Coudenberg, the former Palace of the Count of Flanders, and the Museum of Modern Art next to the Museum of Ancient Art.

The **Museum of Modern Art** is an architectural event in itself. At the centre of a rectangular courtyard between three wings of a former palace of Prince Charles of Lorraine, the museum goes several floors underground. A well of light on two levels creates a unique setting for art display. *See map, fig. 6.*

Since its inauguration in 1984, the museum has attracted international acclaim, both for its revolutionary design and for its collection of 19th and 20th century paintings, mainly by Belgian artists, including the Surrealists René Magritte and Paul Delvaux. Among the non-Belgian artists are Matisse, Gauguin and Dali.

Museum of Ancient Art

The entrance to the adjoining Museum of Ancient Art is in rue de la Régence, in a building opened in 1880. *See Royal Brussels map, fig. 7.*

The centuries move down from earliest at the top, to the 19th and early 20th century on the ground floor. Obviously the museum's greatest and most famous riches are in Flemish and Dutch paintings, especially from the 15th to 17th centuries, with works by Rogier van der Weyden, Memling and Van Dyck.

Rubens has a hall to himself, with some large and magnificent altar paintings. If you want to see work produced by the **Bruegel** family, head for Room 31 on the first floor. Pictures such as the *Census at Bethlehem* or the *Massacre of the Innocents* are biblical only in name. In reality they depict something much more contemporary – the mid-16th century suffering of Flanders under the Spanish yoke.

Bruegel settled in Brussels in 1563 when he married in the church of Notre Dame de la Chapelle; and his two sons, Peter and John, were born here and followed in his artistic footsteps. Peter the Younger especially imitated his father's work.

Rooms 28, 29 and 30 display works by a number of Bruegel's contemporaries – Pieter Baltens, Joachim Beuckelaer and Pieter Aertsen for instance – who show a very similar genre style of crowded village activity, full of character and life, with Biblical scenes in contemporary costume.

Both the Modern and the Ancient Museums are open Tue-Sun 10-17 hrs, but close for lunch.

9.3 Petit and Grand Sablon

Just a few blocks from the Museum of Ancient Art is the charming Square of the Petit Sablon. The little park is surrounded by handsome railings and 48 lively bronze statuettes that represent each of the medieval guilds, crafts and trades.

The statues above the central fountain commemorate the Counts of Egmont and Hornes, heroes of resistance to Spanish rule. They lost their heads in the Grand'Place in 1568. *See map, fig. 8.*

A **Museum of Musical Instruments** is located at number 17 on the square. The full collection runs to 6,000 instruments, for which there is room to display only 500.

In 1997 the museum moves to new premises at Place Royale, in the Villa Hermosa which was formerly the Old England department store, built in Art Nouveau style.

At the top of the square is the 18th-century **Egmont Palace** which was enlarged during the 19th century. *See Royal Brussels map, fig. 9.* It has hosted many famous people including Louis XV, Voltaire and Jean-Jacques Rousseau.

Owned by the Foreign Ministry, it is not open to visitors, but is used for prestigious conferences. In 1972, Britain and Ireland signed up here for membership of the Common Market.

Across the road from Petit Sablon is the church of **Notre Dame des Victoires** – also known as Our Lady of the Sablon. This flamboyant late gothic church was founded in the early 14th century by the guild of crossbowmen. The stained glass windows are superb.

Sloping down beyond the church is the **Place du Grand Sablon**, the heart of the antique dealers district. *See map, fig. 10.* An open-air book and antiques market is held every Saturday and Sunday morning. The square was originally a practice ground for crossbowmen.

Continue further downhill, turn right at the boulevard, and you're within easy reach again of Central Station.

Palais de Justice
At the far end of the rue de la Régence are the enormous Law Courts, which manage to combine just about every architectural style known to man, from Greek and Roman onwards, with overtones of ancient Egypt.

It was the largest building erected in Europe during the 19th century, occupying a much larger acreage than St Peter's in Rome. There's no need to go right up close. The 340-ft dome can be seen from miles away, dominating the city.

9.4 The Cinquantenaire Park

The city's biggest cluster of museums is located at the Cinquantenaire. It's easily reached by Metro from Central Station to Merode (direction Stockel or Herrmann-Debroux). Incidentally, the Metro itself is of great interest to anyone interested in modern Belgian art.

Many of the stations have been decorated by contemporary painters of international calibre. Merode, for instance, where you alight for the Cinquantenaire, features work by artists Roger Raveel and Jean Glibert. A pamphlet called 'Art in the Metro' is available, with recommended itineraries.

The great triumphal archway of the Cinquantenaire was built in 1905, completed rather late to mark the 50th anniversary of Belgium's independence which came in 1830. On top is a Chariot of Victory hauled by four horses. Two curved wings face towards the city, and house the various museums:

Museum of Art & History: global collections from the ancient world of Egypt, Greece and Rome, including a model of 4th-century Rome; the European decorative arts, including tapestries, metal crafts, lace and pottery; and a carriage museum. Open daily except Mon, 9.30-17 hrs on weekdays, 10-17 hrs on weekends. Entrance free.

Museum of Army & Military History: displays all the essential hardware from the armour and swords of medieval times to the more up-to-date world of tanks, bombers and rockets. Open daily except Mon, 9-12 and 13-16.45 hrs. Entrance free.

Autoworld: One of the world's largest and finest car museums, with some 450 vehicles on display. All the great motor names are there: Rochet Schneider, Hispano Suiza, Delhaye. Besides cars, there are posters, engravings and thousands of accessories. Open daily 10-18 hrs Apr-Sep; 10-17 hrs Oct-Mar. Entrance 150 BF.

Chapter Ten
Explore Flanders-on-Sea

The coast of Flanders is only a 15-minute train ride from Bruges. There are several trains every hour to Ostend and another one or two to Blankenberghe or Knokke-Heist (pronounce all the 'k's).

In Bruges the local bus service called the Lijn is based outside the railway station, and serves all coastal destinations.

Ostend is a cheerful resort. You can play golf or tennis, sun-bathe on the sands, or stroll around the harbour filled with international yachts and fishing vessels. The main street called Kapellestraat and its side turnings are pedestrianized. You can eat shrimps, visit a modern art gallery, or go shopping in C&A's.

For lively entertainment, consider spending an evening at Ostend. The Casino comprises a massive leisure centre which includes a concert hall for 2500, a night club featuring top international stars, and European-style roulette with a single zero.

In early March every year, the Casino operates a famed carnival called Bal du Rat Mort (Dead Rat Ball!) for 5000 revellers in fancy dress. More night clubs, discos and singalong cafes are clustered near by.

All the other sandy-beach resorts are within easy range along the flat coastal road. Ostend's major rival is Blankenberghe, 13 miles north. The resort has a long promenade, Casino, pier, yachting harbour and a superb Sea Life Centre filled with North Sea fish.

Family seaside

For a quieter time, turn towards France and explore the resorts of Middelkerke, Westende or La Panne (where sand yachting is a favourite sport). Horse-riders go galloping along the water's edge, or trotting along bridle-paths in the sandy woodlands behind the dunes.

Transport along the entire 40-mile coastline is easily done by tram. Just outside Ostend railway station is the headquarter tram office, where you can buy an all-day ticket costing 330 BF and get a map, timetable and detailed information about each resort.

With the all-day ticket, stop off anywhere, look around, and then continue with a later tram. Every couple of miles there's another family resort, from the French border through to Holland, with Ostend exactly halfway between the two countries.

During the low season, a tram runs every 30 minutes in each direction between the French and Dutch borders. In July and August, frequency rises to every 20 minutes, and every 10 minutes between Nieuwport and Blankenberge from mid-July to around August 20.

Chapter Eleven
The Flemish cuisine

11.1 Reading the menu

Some Flemish menu items need no translation –
Ham, Kotelet, Rosbief Sandwich, Tomaten, Bier,
Koffie, Limonade, Mineraal water, Chocolade,
Jam, Marmelade, Boter, Mayonaise, Peper.

Soups and Starters

Edammer kaaskroketten	Cheese croquettes
Garnalen	Shrimps
Gebonden soep	Cream soup
Heldere soep	Consomme
Ossestaart soep	Oxtail soup
Russisch ei	Russian egg salad
Salade bokaal	Salad bowl
Uiensoep	Onion soup

Main courses and snacks

Biefstuk	Steak
Boerenomelet	Farmer's omelette
Ei	Egg
Forel	Trout
Gehakte biefstuk	Steak tartare
Gebakken mosselen	Fried mussels
Gekookte mosselen	Steamed mussels
Gegrilde vleessoorten	Mixed grill
Gerookte zalm/paling	Smoked salmon/eel
Hutspot	Veg and beef stew
Kaas	Cheese

Koud vlees	Cold meat
Lamsvlees	Lamb
Omelet met ham/kaas	Ham/cheese omelette
Scholfilet	Fillet of flounder
Spek	Bacon
Tong filets	Fillets of sole
Varkensvlees	Pork
Vis	Fish
Vis uit de Rokerij	Assorted smoked fish
Worst	Sausage
Zuurkool met spek en worst	Sauerkraut, bacon and sausage

Vegetables

Aardappelen	Potatoes
Doperwten	Peas
Gebakken aardappelen	Fried potatoes
Groente	Vegetables
Knoflook	Garlic
Prei	Leek
Rijst	Rice
Sla	Salad
Uien	Onions
Witte boon	Butter bean

Desserts

Ananas	Pineapple
Ijs	Ice-cream
Kaasplateau met stokbrood	Cheese board with french bread
Slagroom	Cream
Vanille ijs	Vanilla ice-cream
Vruchten	Fruit salad

Drinks

Appelsap	Apple juice
Koffie met slagroom	Coffee with cream
Melk	Milk
Mineraal water	Mineral water
Sinaasappelsap	Orange juice
Thee	Tea
Thee met citroen	Lemon tea

Tomatensap	Tomato Juice
Wijn: rood / wit	Wine: red / white
Warme chocolademelk	Hot chocolate
(met slagroom)	(with cream)

Miscellaneous

Appelmoes	Apple sauce
Honing	Honey
Noot	Nut
Roomboter	Dairy fresh butter
Slasaus	Salad dressing
Saus	Sauce or gravy
Suiker	Sugar
Zout	Salt

Some Cooking Terms

Gebakken	Fried
Gegratineerd	Au gratin
Gehakt	Chopped
Gekookt	Boiled
Geroosterd	Broiled

Cakes and bread

Appelbol – A whole apple baked in sweet pastry
Brood – Bread, in great variety, including crusty white farmhouse loaves, wholemeal 'boerenbruin', light French 'stokbrood', fruit, nut and muesli breads and banana and apricot loaves.
Chipolata Taart – This is not sausage pie, but a delicious chilled mousse flan
Gosette – A light apple turnover of puff pastry with apple and raisin filling, dusted with sugar.
Kersentaart – Cherry tart
Kwark Taart – Cheese cake
Mocca Gebak – Mocha cake
Roggebrood – Pumpernickel, rye bread
Slagroom Gebak – A pastry shell with a fruit and whipped cream filling
Vruchten Gebak – Fresh fruit flan
Worstebrood – Sausage roll

11.2 Bruges restaurants

You can relax in a traditional tavern and sample the enormous range of Flemish beers, succumb to temptation in chocolate and pastry shops, or settle into a hearty Flemish meal, packed with calories. Belgium is no place for Weightwatchers but you can always diet afterwards. Here's a short list of restaurant suggestions for Bruges.

Duc de Bourgogne, Huidenvettersplein 12. Tel: 332038. *See Bruges map, fig. 6.*
For the splurge of a lifetime in ultra-luxury setting, with very expensive but superlative food. Reckon £25 to £40 for the main course. With wine, figure at least £60 per head. Try for a window seat by the canal.

Den Dyver, Dyver 5. Tel: 336069. *Map, fig. 8.*
Specialises in regional dishes, but all with a beer base or ingredient. Lots of atmosphere; pricey.

Diligence, 50 metres from the Burg (*map, fig. 1*), behind Holiday Inn Hotel. A small tavern with the day's special for about £5: soup, and a large main course. Good beer from the barrel.

Explore the cluster of restaurants along Sint-Amandstraat, just by Market Square (fig. 2).

At reasonable cost, you'll find a Chinese restaurant, several Belgian restaurants and the **Ristorante Italiano**. Equivalent meals on the Market Square itself are always more expensive.

De Stove, Kleine St-Amandstraat 4. Tel: 337835. A small and simple restaurant, right next to the easily-seen Ristorante Italiano. It's operated by a chef who worked years at the Duc de Boulogne, and uses many of the gourmet recipes. There's no view or bow-tie service, but the food is superb at half the Duc de Bourgogne's price.

Chapter Twelve

Go shopping

Most shops are open weekdays 9-18 hrs, with late night shopping on Friday. During winter, shops that sell lace, artwork or antiques are shut on weekdays, but open on Saturday and Sunday 10.30-17:30 hrs.

In Bruges, shops of tourist interest are tightly clustered along the main arteries that radiate from the Market Square. Typical is Wollestraat – Wool Street, a reminder of the trading activity that first brought prosperity to Bruges. But the shopkeepers of Wollestraat sell much more lace, gourmet beer and chocolate than wool.

For general products, the principal shopping streets are Steenstraat and Noordzandstraat, and their side turnings. This area has gained shopping prominence mainly since the 19th century when the railway station changed the travel pattern of people who arrived in town. Formerly the main shopping street was Vlamingstraat, which runs north from Market Square.

For local character and colour, visit the street markets that operate 7-13 hrs on Wednesday in the Burg Square, Saturday at 't Zand and Beursplein, and daily except Sunday in the Fish Market (Vis-Markt). Major supermarkets are banished to locations outside the city centre, but there are several shopping galleries.

12.2 What to buy

Shops focus on high quality rather than low price. Shoes, for instance, come in a range of 3,300 to 7,000 BF – way over £160, or £80 as starters. Just face the fact that the exchange rate is not particularly attractive for the English pound or even the US dollar.

Lace: At last count, Bruges had 53 lace shops. It may seem like more, but that's mainly because they are tightly concentrated along the lines of tourist movement. For centuries lace-making in Bruges was a traditional pin-money activity of working women, seeking to augment the family income. On sunny days around thirty years ago, you could still see old ladies sitting outside their front doors, clicking away at their bobbins.

Today that sight is a rarity. Demonstrations are given in some of the lace shops, or every weekday afternoon at the Kantcentrum Lace Centre in Balstraat. But the pupils of the craft school today are principally the wives or daughters of professional people who take up lace-making as a genteel hobby. Working women find more rewarding employment.

Meanwhile, most of the annual three million visitors to Bruges want to buy at least one souvenir lace handkerchief. Plainly, if they had to satisfy that demand, the lace-makers of Bruges wouldn't have any fingers left. So it's Taiwan to the rescue, keeping the lace shops well stocked with beautifully-made products.

The only way you can tell the difference between genuine Brussels or Bruges hand-made lace and Taiwan machine-made is in the price. A superb tablecloth – a future family heirloom – can cost £800 or even £1,000. But you can always buy at lower cost, thanks to Taiwan.

Typical prices: a lace bra for £23 or OS for £30; bookmarks for £3; little table mats for £2.50; gloves for £7; knickers for £17.

Chocolates: Belgian chocolates have a high reputation for quality. This is due to very strict legislation enacted in 1870, defining chocolate as a blend of cocoa beans, sugar and nothing else. Only products which respected this definition could be sold as chocolate, forcing confectioners to abandon cheap ingredients and seek success in high quality.

Hence a brisk demand in Bruges and Brussels which support as many confectionary stores as lace shops. All these chocolate shops feature mouth-watering displays of chocolates in many peculiar shapes and designs, besides nougat, marzipan and hand-made pralines. Reckon about £10 a kilo, or £5 a pound.

Pralines – usually a creamy mixture with nuts, coated with chocolate – were invented in the 17th century by a chef working for a French count called Plessis-Praslin, who gave his name to the confection.

The choice of delicate flavoured fillings is infinite. Some pralines even contain liqueur. These are highly appreciated by connoisseurs who say that the sweet taste of the liqueur blends perfectly with the bitterness of pure chocolate.

Caution! Sometimes people come to Bruges on a day trip, rush in to buy half a kilo of pralines and then at the end of a hot summer's day they have one praline weighing a pound. It's better to let pralines melt in your mouth.

Beer: In a land of dedicated beer drinkers, Belgium offers three or four hundred different brews, each having its loyal fans. It's all part of the Belgian beer culture.

To help visitors take the happy memories back home, beer-souvenir shops sell presentation mini-crates of bottled beer, each demanding its specialised drinking glass.

A car driver could load his boot with several hundred bottles, all different, without protest from the UK Customs.

Diamonds: Antwerp claims to be the world's largest diamond centre, accounting for 54% of the global production of cut diamonds, putting the city well ahead of Amsterdam. The industry produces an annual turnover of £16 billion – 7% in value of Belgium's exports.

The Antwerp diamond district facing Central Station has been traditionally 'off limits' to anyone outside the trade. But an exhibition centre called Diamondland now enables visitors to see craftsmen at work and to learn all about diamonds. Jewellery is offered at competitive prices.

Diamondland is located at Appelmansstraat 33a very close to Antwerp's Central Station. Open Mon-Sat 9.30-17.30 hrs, entrance free.

According to recent research, Bruges was the centre of a brisk diamond trade already in 1372, long before Antwerp and Amsterdam established their industry. Also in Bruges, the technique of diamond polishing on a rotating disk was developed over 500 years ago by a local goldsmith.

Brugs Diamanthuis at Cordoeaniersstraat 5 (a hundred yards from Market Square) is a splendid jewellery showroom established in a mansion called 'de Stuer' (the Sturgeon). The Diamond House gives demonstrations of traditional diamond cutting, but only on Saturdays.

Antiques: Bruges and Brussels are something like clearing houses for antiques. At the budget end of the market, a flea market in Bruges is held beside the canal at Dijver during the March-October season on weekend afternoons. The Grand Sablon square in Brussels likewise features an open-air antiques market at weekends.

An extra attraction for autumn visitors to Bruges is a week-long annual International Antiques Fair in late October/early November. The Fair is held in the Medieval Halls and Inner Court of the Belfry. Flemish and international antiques include glass, china, jewellery, silver, clocks, tapestries, furniture and paintings.

Chapter Thirteen
At your service

Changing money

The Belgian Franc (abbreviated as BF) is one of
Europe's hard currencies, and stands firm on the
exchanges. Reckon 45 BF to the pound, or 30 BF
to the US dollar. Exchange bureau or bank commis-
sions always ensure that the final outcome is somewhat less.

Banks usually give the best deal, open 9-16 hrs
Mon-Fri, which is no use for anyone on a weekend
trip. However, all the major credit cards are uni-
versally accepted, and their final exchange rate is
reasonable.

Costs

Mostly you'll find Belgium a bit more expensive
than Britain. Partly that depends on whether sterling
is currently strong or weak. It's also the result of
higher income-levels in Belgium, and a rate of
20.5% VAT. But the difference is not big enough
to be a deterrent to UK visitors.

Belgium generally is not a bargain-hunters' para-
dise, and dedicated shoppers have picked the wrong
country.

Because all the sightseeing highlights are so tightly grouped together, everything worth seeing in
Bruges is within walking distance. Whichever zig-
zag route you take is part of the scenic enjoyment.
Transport costs inside Bruges are minimal, except
for a £4 or £5 taxi each way between railway station and hotel.

Entrances to the major museums cost around £3
a time; smaller museums £1 or £1.50.

Mealtime
Restaurant prices are higher than in Britain, but portions are hefty. A starter and main course at lunchtime leave most people with no room for dessert. Many restaurants offer set lunches at around £6. For around £2 a well-filled ham or cheese roll with salad is the basis for a lunchtime picnic.

What to pack
The weather is very similar to Britain's. During winter, spring and autumn, be prepared with warm clothing. Even in summer, have a sweater in reserve. Forget about high heels, with all those cobbles. Comfortable, flat footwear is much better.

If you want to use any electric gadgets, pack a plug adaptor. Belgium is on 220 volts, but uses the Continental-type 2-pin plug.

Don't worry if your cosmetic, pharmaceutical or film supplies run out. All the major brands are readily available in Bruges. A chemist's shop is *Apotheek*.

Tipping
In restaurants and cafés, 15% service is automatically included in the bill, but it's usual to leave any small change.

Local time
Simple enough in summer and winter, Belgium is one hour ahead of UK. But Britain does not synchronise with Western Europe on the changeover dates to and from summer time.

Be extra cautious about time differences and airline schedules in March and in September/October - especially at weekends when either Europe or Britain is changing the clocks.

Safety and Security
Risks are minimal. Belgium's crime rate is among the lowest in Europe, and is mainly concentrated in some areas of Brussels. However, it's sensible not to make things easy for pickpockets. Leave any bulk supplies of money in your hotel safe-deposit.

Daily Hours

Most shops are open weekdays 9-18 hrs, with late night shopping on Friday. Some tourist shops are open Sundays.

The principal museums operate 9.30-17.00 daily during the Apr-Sep high season; but close for lunch from 12 or 12.30 till 14.00 hrs during the Oct-Mar off-season. Nothing's open on Christmas Day or New Year's Day. On other public holidays, most museums are open.

Evening mealtimes start around 6 p.m., and restaurants often are taking last orders by 10 p.m. Bars are open till past midnight if there are customers still around.

Post and telephone

Letters and postcards to Britain and other EU countries cost 16 BF. To avoid the usual hotel markups, buy a 200-franc phone card which can give you a decent chat with the folks back home.

Learn some Flemish

In Belgium, half the population speak French, but the northern half speak Flemish, which doubles as Dutch – in the same way that American has some resemblance to English.

Really, there's not the slightest need to learn any Dutch, as it's hard to find anyone who doesn't have at least basic English. But some elementary Dutch is very easy to pick up - particularly if you already know German!

Dutch is rather like a stepping-stone between German and English. Words are glued together, as in German, so that street-names for instance can look terrifying. But they're really quite simple when you break the monster words down into their component parts. Grammar is simpler, closer to English; and there are no accents to bother about.

Listed below are some simple words and phrases for those who like going local.

Yes / No	Ja / Neé
Good morning	Goede morgen
Good afternoon	Goede middag

Goodbye	Tot ziens!
How are you?	Hoe gaat het met uw?
Please	Alstublieft
Thank you	Dank u wel / Bedankt
How much	Hoeveel kost?
I am hungry / thirsty	Ik heb honger / dorst
Breakfast	Ontbijt
Dinner	Avondeten
Sandwich	Broodje
Cup of coffee / tea	Kepje koffie / thee
Dish of the day	Dagschotel
May I have the bill	Mag ik afrekenen
A ticket to…	Een kaartje naar…
One-way ticket	Enkele reis
Return	Retour
Ticket office	Loket
Postcard	Briefkaart
Telephone booth	Telefooneel
Push / Pull	Duwen / Trekken
Hot / Cold	Warm / Koud
Entrance / Exit	Ingang / Uitgang
Emergency exit	Nooduitgang
Left / Right	Links / rechts
No smoking	Niet roken
Exchange office	Wisselkantoor
I come from England	Ik kom uit Engeland

Dual place names

Somewhat confusing for visitors, many Belgian cities have alternate versions of their names, Flemish or French. Often, too, the cities are spelt differently in English! Here's a selection:

English	Flemish	French
Antwerp	Antwerpen	Anvers
Bruges	Brugge	Bruges
Brussels	Brussel	Bruxelles
Courtrai	Kortrijk	Courtrai
Ghent	Gent	Gand
La Panne	De Panne	La Panne
Liege	Luik	Liège
Ostend	Oostende	Ostende
Ypres	Ieper	Ypres

Public holidays

Shops, banks and offices are closed on:
January 1; Easter Monday; May 1; Ascension Day;
Whit Monday; July 11; July 21; August 15
Assumption Day; early November, All Saints Day;
November 11 Armistice Day; 25 December.

Addresses and phone numbers

Belgian Tourist Office, 29 Princes Street, London
W1R 7RG. Tel: 0891-887799 (Premium charges
apply).

Belgian Tourist Office, 780 Third Avenue, Suite
1501, New York, NY 10017. Tel: 212-758-8130.
Fax: 212-355-7675.

Belgian National Railways, 10 Greycoat Place,
London SW1. Tel: 0891-516444 (Premium charge).
A recorded information and brochure-request line is
0891-887799 (39p per minute cheap rate, 49p at
other times).

SABENA Belgian World Airlines, 10 Putney Hill,
London SW15. Tel: 0181-780 1444.

EUROSTAR Tel: 01233-617575.

Tourist Information Bureaux:

Antwerp: Grote Markt 15. Tel: 03/232-0103.
Bruges: Burg 11. Tel: 050/448686.
Brussels: Stadhuis (Town Hall), Grand'Place. Tel:
02/513-8940.
Ghent: Crypte Stadhuis (Town Hall), Botermarkt.
Tel: 09/266-5232.
Ostend: Monacoplein 2. Tel: 059/701199.

Emergency phone: Police dial 101; ambulance dial
100.